PRAISE FOR
THE FAITH OF ELVIS

"You haven't met the real Elvis if you haven't read The Faith of Elvis. Billy Stanley shows us a side of the King we've never seen before—an older brother, mentor, and follower of Jesus. Prepare to be blown away by a whole new glimpse into one of the greatest performers of all time."

—MIKE HUCKABEE, HOST OF THE *HUCKABEE* SHOW

"Billy Stanley's *The Faith of Elvis* gives you an inside look at an Elvis that few really knew, but all can learn from. It is a story that only a brother can share and reveals Elvis's love for God and his savior Jesus Christ. Billy delivers a beautiful, true account filled with passion and hope that captures the true essence of Elvis's life and his love for God and his fans."

—DAVID E. STANLEY, STEPBROTHER TO ELVIS
PRESLEY, AUTHOR, AND PRODUCER

"Everyone needs a mentor and someone to guide us when our faith is young. What a joy to know that Elvis understood the value of investing in the faith of those he loved."

—JOHN STANGE, HOST OF THE POPULAR *CHAPTER-A-DAY AUDIO
BIBLE* PODCAST AND AUTHOR OF *DWELL ON THESE THINGS*

"To know Elvis the star and the icon is a thrill and to learn of Elvis the man and the brother is pure joy. A further glimpse into his powerful spiritual side takes it up another notch still. Billy Stanley's The Faith of Elvis gives us that firsthand personal perspective. Just as music and love are to be shared, faith and commitment to God through Jesus Christ are a part of Elvis Presley that he willingly imparted through his life and actions. Who better to describe this side of the man, than the brother who lived alongside him for seventeen years? While Elvis's passion comes through, so does Billy's. I wholeheartedly recommend this worthwhile read. It's a must for those who seek to know the essence behind the glitter."

—JANET BOSTIC, HEAD WRITER AT TCB RADIO AND ADMINISTRATOR OF
THE ELVIS: A CELEBRATION OF THE MAN AND HIS MUSIC FAN CLUB

THE FAITH OF ELVIS

THE FAITH OF
ELVIS

A Story Only a Brother Can Tell

Billy Stanley

with Kent Sanders

NELSON
BOOKS

An Imprint of Thomas Nelson

ISBN 978-1-4002-3704-3 (TP)
ISBN 978-1-4002-3702-9 (eBook)
ISBN 978-1-4002-3700-5 (HC)

Library of Congress Control Number: 2022939077

Printed in the United States of America
23 24 25 26 27 LBC 5 4 3 2 1

First and foremost, I want to thank God
for the story he has given me.

This book is dedicated to:

Elvis, for accepting me into his family and
teaching me about the Lord.

Rick and David Stanley, for showing me
a better life though the Lord.

My mother, for taking me to church,
even when I didn't want to go.

The fans, for loving my brother, Elvis.

And, last but not least, my wife, Liz. God brought us back together
for a reason, and that reason is to share how great God really is
and to show everyone that God does have plans for them. Just
be patient and wait for all of the blessings that he has for you.

CONTENTS

Introduction   xi

PART 1: FAITH LIKE A CHILD

Chapter 1:   Mansion Over the Hilltop   3

Chapter 2:   He Knows Just What I Need   13

Chapter 3:   You'll Never Walk Alone   23

Chapter 4:   In My Father's House   31

Chapter 5:   Somebody Bigger Than You and I   39

Chapter 6:   I'll Be Home for Christmas   47

Chapter 7:   It Is No Secret (What God Can Do)   55

Chapter 8:   He Touched Me   63

Chapter 9:   Oh Happy Day   67

PART 2: THE HOPE OF HIS CALLING

Chapter 10:   Where No One Stands Alone   77

Chapter 11:   By and By   83

Chapter 12:   Stand by Me   91

Chapter 13:   I've Got Confidence   99

Chapter 14:   Swing Down, Sweet Chariot   109

CONTENTS

Chapter 15:   Lead Me, Guide Me   117

Chapter 16:   If the Lord Wasn't Walking by My Side   125

Chapter 17:   America, the Beautiful   133

Chapter 18:   Run On   141

PART 3: THE GREATEST OF THESE IS LOVE

Chapter 19:   How Great Thou Art   151

Chapter 20:   Amazing Grace   157

Chapter 21:   Help Me   165

Chapter 22:   Farther Along   173

Chapter 23:   Known Only to Him   181

Chapter 24:   If We Never Meet Again   191

Chapter 25:   Seeing Is Believing   197

Chapter 26:   A Thing Called Love   209

The Faith of Elvis *Discussion Guide*   217

Acknowledgments   233

Notes   235

About the Authors   237

INTRODUCTION

Elvis is alive. I know it sounds crazy, but it's true. How do I know he's alive? Because I've seen him.

As I watched Elvis's casket being placed into a mausoleum in 1977, I felt an overwhelming grief, assuming I would never see him again. But I did see him. The first time was in a dream ten years later. Drugs and bad decisions had brought me to the lowest point in my life, and the words he spoke changed my life forever.

I saw Elvis a second time in 2018, forty-one years after he died. I suffered a major heart attack and was clinically dead for ten minutes. But it was enough time to see Elvis in a vision. We talked briefly, and he shared his final message with me: "Tell all of my family, friends, and fans I love them. And I'll see them when they get here."

This book is not just my attempt to share the message Elvis gave to me. I also want to reveal the true story of a great man.

Behind the glitz and glamour, beyond the movies and millions of records sold, is a man driven by his faith in God. I didn't know him as a fan, a Hollywood producer, or the countless number of people who wanted a piece of him. I knew him as a brother.

I want you to see the man who gave so much of himself—almost too much. A man who thought it was better to give than to receive. A man dedicated to protecting his younger brothers and sharing the love of Jesus with each of us.

This is a story of faith, hope, and love. It is a story only a brother can tell.

∽

I was seven years old when my mother, Dee, brought me and my two younger brothers to live at Graceland in 1960. Although my brother Ricky and I were born the same year, in 1953, I was older than him for eleven months out of the year. I was born in January and he was born in December. My brother David was two years younger.

As for my mother, she was still young in years but long in life experience. As a military wife who had moved around a lot, she was ready to settle down. My mother and father were separated, but their divorce was not finalized. She would go on to marry Elvis's father, Vernon, a few months after we moved in with the Presley family.

None of us had any idea how our lives were about to change. Moments after we arrived at Graceland, the man the world knew as "the King" scooped me and my brothers up in his arms and exclaimed, "Daddy, I always wanted a little brother. Now I've got three!" These were some of the first words I ever heard Elvis speak.

He would never call us stepbrothers. From that moment forward, we were simply his *brothers*. We were a family.

We were only children when we arrived, pulled into a world the three of us could never have imagined. Elvis instantly stepped in as any older brother would and cared for us. Through the years, countless people came in and out of Elvis's life. But we were there through it all, on the inside, with the real Elvis. He became our friend, mentor, guide, teacher, and cheerleader. No one had more impact on me and my brothers' lives.

For as long as I can remember, Elvis used the same Bible, which went with him everywhere. When I was finally old enough to work for him, I was in charge of that Bible. I made sure the Bible made it to every hotel room where he stayed. I placed it neatly on his bedside table, where he wanted it to be waiting for him before and after his sold-out performances.

For years, when he would call me to his room, Elvis would be holding his Bible in his hands when I arrived. It was well-worn, filled with his own notes and highlights. I was a young man, thrust into a world that was constantly under the spotlight, and he entrusted me with that Bible to guard and ensure it was everywhere he went. In those private moments when he spent time with his Bible, I saw the real Elvis, a man rooted in faith.

From the day we met until our last conversation, he shared that faith with me. It began with a special bedtime prayer our first night at Graceland and ended just two days before his death in a conversation about Jesus, love, and forgiveness. In the seventeen years between, I was a firsthand witness to his faith in Jesus and love for everyone.

Elvis wasn't perfect. Just like the rest of us who walk this earth, he was broken. Even so, Elvis knew he was blessed, and he loved to give to others. He extended the same generosity to everyone. His message was always clear: treat everyone the same. Look at their hearts and souls, how they treat you. Even if they treat you badly, something could be going on in their lives at the time. So, you just look at them and say, "I forgive you," and go on.

Elvis believed in love and wanted that for me and my brothers more than anything. He wanted that for everyone. He lived it every day and found a way to share it with the world through his life and music.

There came a time in Elvis's career when he began including a gospel set in his show. Thousands of adoring fans, seeking the thrill of his signature music, were introduced to his version of gospel songs and hymns. This was his testimony. He saw his music as a way not just to make a living, but to change lives. He saw it as a ministry.

Elvis knew he couldn't perform miracles, but miracles happened through the power of his music. He was spreading the good news with the gift God gave him, his voice. The stage was his pulpit. The screaming fans were his congregation. And it was magical.

Fans would come up to us, talking about how the gospel set made them believe again. They came to see "the King," but left knowing another King, the One who could save them. This was his legacy.

Elvis released two dozen albums in different genres over his career. But he only won Grammy Awards for his gospel music. If you listen to his recordings of gospel songs, you can hear there is something different, something more soulful about those recordings. The reason is because those songs contained a truth that reached more deeply into Elvis's soul than anything else.

His favorite Bible verse was John 3:16, which says, "For God so loved the world that he gave his one and only Son, that whoever believes in him shall not perish but have eternal life." That is what Elvis wanted more than anything: for people to know God and come to faith in Jesus.

Elvis sensed that his time on earth was limited. Shortly before his death, he sat down with the three of us, his brothers. He said, "If anything happens to me, if I die, there's only three people in this world who can truly tell my story from the right perspective. As my brothers, you're the only ones who can do that."

Now it's time to carry that torch, to see through the wishes of the King of Rock and Roll.

∞

Why another Elvis book among the countless others that have been written? Because there is a side of Elvis that has not been explored until now: his faith. I told the story of my life with Elvis in my previous book, *Elvis,*

My Brother. Now I'm ready to share my firsthand perspective of Elvis's true motivation: to share God's love through his life and music.

The book is mostly chronological, but not strictly so, since each chapter focuses on a specific topic related to Elvis's faith. Many of the chapters focus on themes directly related to notes and reminders Elvis wrote in his Bible. Sharp-eyed Elvis fans will notice that most of the chapter titles are gospel songs recorded by Elvis.

The book is divided into three parts, based on the trifecta of "faith, hope and love" from 1 Corinthians 13:13.

Part 1, "Faith Like a Child," explores my early days with Elvis when he was helping my faith develop. In many ways, he was a big kid at heart. These chapters focus on topics such as his family, his music and his relationship with his fans, how he mentored me and my brothers, and how he dealt with fame.

Part 2, "The Hope of His Calling," explores the conflicts, opportunities, and stories related to different areas of Elvis's life as his faith was put to the test. These chapters include topics such as his support of racial equality, his love of cars, his struggle to transition from movies back to concerts, and his impromptu visit with President Nixon.

Part 3, "The Greatest of These Is Love," takes us to even greater depths of Elvis's faith. You will hear stories about his use of gospel music in concerts, his struggle with fame, and his suspicions that he might die young. You will also get firsthand accounts of my spiritual encounters with Elvis since his death.

The story of Elvis isn't just a story of music or fame. It is a story reminding the world that we are all worthy of redemption and grace. And what better place for three young boys to learn that lesson than in a place called Graceland?

PART 1

FAITH LIKE A CHILD

ONE

MANSION OVER THE HILLTOP

I remember the first time I heard the name Elvis Presley. We were sitting around the dinner table and my father nonchalantly said, "Private Presley checked in today." You'd have thought he was reciting a random fact he'd heard on the news instead of the earthshaking information it was to most Americans.

It was 1959, and we were living in Germany, where my father, Bill, was stationed. Elvis was stationed at the same base, and my father and Elvis's father, Vernon, had become friends. My father was a career sergeant, and the Army was his life. He was not a pleasant person to be around, and neither me nor my brothers had much of a relationship with him. According to my mother, my father was not happy unless there was a war.

My father was also an alcoholic who had turned to the bottle to manage his pain. I remember him telling me years later, "Billy, nobody ever survives war. I don't care if they come home or not." My father may have

3

"come home" from the war, but he did not emotionally survive, especially after seeing his best friend's head get blown off.

He and my mother became more distant over time, especially when Vernon entered the picture. Vernon's wife, Gladys, had died the year before. I saw Vernon a few times at our house in Germany, and he and my mother would talk on the phone quite a bit when my father was gone. When my father was home, he would go out with Vernon and sometimes my mom would join them. Odd as it sounds, pretty soon my father asked Vernon to take her out because he couldn't do it.

As a widower, Vernon was drawn to my mother's energy and charm. She was a petite blonde with blue eyes and excellent cooking skills. He started seeing my mom regularly and said that he wanted to marry her. By that point, my parents had already decided to get a divorce. That was no surprise because their arguments had gotten worse than usual, especially since Vernon had entered the picture. It was just a matter of time until Vernon would become our stepfather.

Elvis was a worldwide sensation by this time. However, Vernon was the one who was much more prominent in my life when we lived in Germany. He would mention things like, "I've got a son named Elvis." It was never, "I've got a son who is a famous rock and roll musician" or "He's a movie star." Before meeting Elvis, I never thought of him as being anyone other than Vernon's son.

Vernon knew that Elvis was going to come back to the States in 1960 after his Army commitment was finished. As a result, he and my mother wanted to get us kids back here before then and return to Germany to get the divorce finalized since my father was remaining there. Vernon took us to the airport in his car, and there was no discussion of what was going on. Kids back then were seen but not heard, so we just sat there and didn't ask questions.

My main memory from the airport was that it looked like something out of *Casablanca*, in the final scene, when Ingrid Bergman is about to get on the plane. It was a foggy German night, and I remember walking up the airplane steps. When I got to the top, I turned around to look and there were two men, Vernon and my father. My life was changing right before my eyes. One man was coming into the picture, and the other was going out.

My mother needed to arrange temporary housing for us boys for a few months since she didn't own a residence in the States. The best she could do was arrange for us to stay with our aunt Peggy. However, she only had a trailer and already had her two teenagers living with her. We only stayed there about a month.

Vernon located a boarding school and arranged for our stay there. When we arrived, the staff showed us all around and told us how great it would be. They even took us for a boat ride to make it seem like a happy place. But as soon as Vernon and my mother left to head back to Germany, things got dark pretty fast.

The headmistress took us into our room and pointed out, "That's where you'll be sleeping." She told us not to ask any questions and just stay in line. When the staff corrected us, they never whipped us, but instead put Tabasco sauce on our tongues. That happened to me a lot. At the time, it burned, but over the years I came to enjoy Tabasco. Crazy, huh?

During Halloween, I remember the older kids saying, "You younger kids stay inside, and we'll come and get you later." I thought that was kind of strange but assumed maybe that was the way they did it there.

I was lying in my bed, which just happened to be right next to a window with blinds. I pulled the blinds up and looked outside. I could see all the older kids dressed up in their costumes, getting into cars. They never came back to take us. But that's what it was like there. The older kids got everything and we didn't get anything.

Looking back on it now, I understand that our mother was doing the best with what she had. She knew the boarding school was a temporary arrangement and that we had a much better life ahead if we could just be patient. She had no idea that the dog and pony show put on by the staff when we arrived was the complete opposite of what it was actually like. From our perspective as kids, we felt like our mother had abandoned us. We got a phone call every now and then. "I'll come pick you boys up as soon as I can get there." But that was it. This went on for four or five months. We wondered if we had done something wrong.

The real kicker came during the Christmas season. We saw all the other kids leaving with their families for the holidays. But not us. There was only one other kid who was left there for Christmas. Nobody came to pick us up, take us home, or bring any gifts. We didn't understand what was happening or what a divorce was. All we knew was that we were alone.

At age six, I didn't know anything about prayer. But that's when I said my first one, there at the boarding school. I cried, "Please, Lord, get us out of here. What did we do to deserve this?"

I had no way of knowing that around the same time, Elvis was finishing his service in the Army. My mother traveled back to the States with him and took the train to Memphis. One day she called us at the school and told us she would pick us up in a few days to take us to our new home. We were excited yet apprehensive following the last several months. Last time we were promised a sleepaway camp, and look how that turned out!

We packed up our few belongings with no idea what to expect. The morning we were to be picked up, the staff had us dress up in our best clothes. When our mother arrived, we walked outside and saw a brand-new, shiny, black Lincoln Continental. It was the biggest car I had ever seen in my life.

"Where's Dad?" David asked Mom.

"You boys know Vernon. He is going to be your new father."

We didn't understand what was happening, but we did know one thing: we couldn't get out of there fast enough. We piled into the back seat and headed toward our new home in Memphis.

It was a chilly night in March 1960 when our Lincoln pulled up to the wrought iron gates of Graceland. My two younger brothers and I had fallen asleep on the way. Mom was excitedly reaching into the back seat, telling us, "Wake up, boys! Wake up, boys! This is your new home."

Vernon honked the horn and the magical gates slowly opened to our new life. I rubbed my eyes in disbelief as I stared wide-eyed through the windshield. We rolled gently by giant musical notes and the silhouette of a man playing guitar built into the gates. The house was lit up from the outside. It looked like a castle straight out of a Disney movie. My world instantly turned from black and white into a Technicolor dream brighter and more beautiful than anything I had seen on television.

"Does a king live here?" I asked.

"Some people say he's a king," Vernon replied.

I couldn't wrap my mind around the size of the house. My father was in the military, and we were accustomed to small apartments. A big home to us meant one that had two or three bedrooms. Pulling into the driveway at Graceland, I realized this castle would be my new home. And it definitely had more than three bedrooms.

As soon as the car stopped, me and my brothers spilled out into the driveway. We were led through the back door of the house and instantly embraced by Alberta, one of the maids at Graceland. A large, loving, Black woman who immediately made us feel welcomed and important, she had a smile that could light up a room. When she hugged you, it made everything disappear. She was the first person we met, and with a big smile on her face, she said, "I'm gonna treat these boys like my own!"

Alberta told us that Elvis was waiting for us downstairs, playing pool. We nervously descended the stairs and entered an unknown, dimly lit, smoky room with a group of people crowded around a pool table. We stood there at the entrance, unsure if we should approach the table. It grew quiet, and then a deep voice with an unmistakable southern accent said, "Eight ball, corner pocket." I heard the sound of the balls striking and the soft thud of the eight ball landing home. The crowd cheered and applauded.

Someone hollered, "Nice shot, E!"

Almost on cue, the crowd parted like the seas and turned to us. There, at the other end, stood Elvis. It seemed as if a spotlight shone on him with a pool cue in hand, eyes fixed on us. His face lit up as he set down his cue and walked across the room.

Looking down at the three of us, he asked, "What do we have here, Daddy?"

Vernon smiled and held his hand out as if presenting us. "These are your new brothers, Elvis."

Without waiting to even hear his father finish his presentation, Elvis leaned down and scooped all three of us up in his arms. I could feel the love coming from him. He had been expecting us. He knew we were scared and overwhelmed. I felt protected for the first time in many months. While still squeezing the three of us, he said, "Daddy, I always wanted a little brother, and now I have three!"

In the span of twelve hours, we had gone from being seemingly abandoned to the loving embrace of Elvis, safely inside the walls of the castle known as Graceland. We were in uncharted territory and had no idea what to expect. But from the moment we encountered Alberta, it felt like home.

Elvis turned to Vernon. "Daddy, I'm sure you and Dee are tired from the trip. Why don't you guys do what you want to do, and I'll tuck in the boys?" Vernon agreed and the crowd left us alone in the pool room with our new big brother.

Elvis asked us all kinds of questions about what kind of toys we liked and what we were interested in. After a couple of hours, he led us upstairs to get ready for bed. We were excited to be in our new home with our new older brother and quickly got our pajamas on and brushed our teeth. Elvis stood there, smiling and laughing at us.

"Are you ready to go to bed?" Elvis asked.

"Yup!"

"Haven't you forgotten something?"

"We already brushed our teeth!"

"No. You forgot to say your prayers."

The three of us had only ever said prayers at mealtime, so this was foreign to us. But we followed our big brother's lead, knelt with him at the end of the bed, and folded our hands in prayer. Elvis spoke this prayer on our first night: "Dear heavenly Father, we thank you for this day and for our many blessings. I want to thank you for bringing these three little boys into my life. I promise to love and protect them for the rest of my life."

I looked up at him as he finished his prayer and was in awe of this amazing man. He was like no one I had ever met. Nobody had ever said a prayer like that for us before. I reached up and put my hand on his back. He looked down and a tear came to his eye. He picked us up one at a time, tossed us in bed, and gave us each a kiss on the cheek.

I fell asleep that night in wonder.

❧

The next morning, we were awakened by Elvis excitedly running around the room, yelling at us to get up. "We've gotta go outside! We've gotta go outside!" I tried to shake off the sleepiness and locate my clothes.

Elvis yelled, "No time for that!" He scooped up David and threw him over his shoulders, grabbed Ricky and me, and ran us outside to the backyard.

What we found in the yard was the most amazing sight my seven-year-old eyes had ever seen. We stood in awe of a yard full of all the toys you could possibly imagine. Bikes, cars, balls, you name it. Three of each one. I thought to myself, *This guy is Santa Claus.* It turned out that after he put us to bed the night before, Elvis had stores in Memphis open up just for him. He went and bought all those toys based on the answers we had given him while hanging out around the pool table.

I was frozen, and so were Ricky and David. I said, "Whose are those?"

Elvis said, "They're yours!"

"Can we play with them?"

"Yes. They're yours. You can go play with them!"

And we did. We ran through the yard, exploring all the new, amazing toys. Elvis ran with us, horsing around and helping when necessary. I gravitated to one of the bikes. It had training wheels on it, but I let him know I didn't need them. Someone grabbed him a wrench and he started to take them off, but I jumped in to show him I could do it myself.

"Oh, a mechanic too?" Elvis said, laughing.

I removed the training wheels and tried to swing my leg over the seat. It was too high and a little tough to get going on the grass in the backyard at Graceland, so Elvis held the seat while I mounted the bike. He ran behind me as I pedaled up to speed.

We spent the rest of the day playing in the yard. As the day turned to night and the hours passed, we eventually went back inside and got dressed. Elvis pulled me aside and said, "Now I want to show you some of my toys!" He led me to the garage.

I couldn't believe his collection of cars. I recognized the black four-door Lincoln Continental we had traveled in the day before. There was also his iconic 1955 pink Cadillac Fleetwood and a white two-door Lincoln Continental Mark II. And of course, his Harley-Davidson motorcycle.

But the vehicles that interested me most were two racing go-karts.

My eyes opened wide, and Elvis helped me sit in one of them to try it out. He said, "One day I'll teach you how to drive it."

I got out of the go-kart, and we walked to the end of the line of parked vehicles, where I saw one more car. However, this one wasn't a full-sized automobile or a go-kart. It was a smaller, red, battery-operated car. I asked who it belonged to, and he explained that it was just for me. I was so excited I could hardly stand it. I asked if I could sit in it. Elvis was laughing as he said again that the car was mine.

He sat me in the car and we started talking. I said how excited I was to finally learn how to drive. He told me that he was going to be the one to teach me how to drive. He explained, "Billy, the right pedal makes it go. The left pedal makes it stop." Elvis also said that eventually he would teach me how to race cars!

As a seven-year-old, this was music to my ears.

∽

Those first twenty-four hours at Graceland were the things dreams are made of. Not because we had arrived at a house that seemed as large as a castle or had been given more toys than we'd ever seen at one time. It was because we felt abundant love. We knew we were protected.

As a person of faith, it's easy to talk the talk instead of walking the walk. But deeds are more powerful than words. Elvis didn't just sing about the gospel—he lived it. James 1:22–24 says, "Do not merely listen to the word, and so deceive yourselves. Do what it says. Anyone who listens to the word but does not do what it says is like someone who looks at his face in a mirror and, after looking at himself, goes away and immediately forgets what he looks like."

When I read the Bible, I see a God of love. Elvis was a living, breathing example of God's love. We didn't know Elvis as the world knew him. The day before, he had been a stranger to us. We had no idea how famous he was or that he was a movie star. He was just a man who welcomed us into his home and treated us like his own kids. He prayed with us. Played with us. And would provide for us and protect us.

Elvis sang an old gospel song about a "mansion over the hilltop." He wasn't kidding. It wasn't just a home that he bought, and it wasn't just the place I grew up in as a kid. It's also the one God has waiting for us in heaven.

TWO

HE KNOWS JUST
WHAT I NEED

In my collection of photos, there is one taken at Graceland in October 1960. From the look of things, my brothers and I were playing cowboys and Indians near the gates that day. We didn't normally play near the gates, but someone must have yelled for us to come over.

That wasn't unusual. Elvis's fans often yelled for us to come to them whenever they saw us playing in the yard. The first question they would always ask is, "What are you doing here, kid?" My answer was always the same. "I live here." Graceland was the first real home we ever had.

That photo captures a defining moment in our young lives. We were on the inside looking out at the world. The view we had was unbelievable.

It wasn't about the mansion, the cars, or the toys. It was about the family. God knew that what my brothers and I needed more than anything was a stable, secure family who could lead us to Jesus. And at the center of this family was Elvis. The person you saw on the screen or at concerts was the same person you saw at Graceland. Elvis was every bit the fun-loving, warm, caring person you'd expect him to be, and then some.

In that setting of a secure and loving family, we began to learn more about Jesus.

❦

After we moved to Graceland, my mother made sure we were in church every time the doors were open. That was two times on Sunday and once on Wednesday. Whitehaven Church of Christ was practically our second home. From 1960 to 1969, I was there at every service, vacation Bible school, or event. My mother even enrolled us in the Christian school they had.

One day the pastor asked if anyone had any questions. I raised my hand and said, "I have a friend who goes to the Baptist church—"

The pastor interrupted me and said, "Well, he's going to hell."

I was completely confused because I had learned that you shouldn't pass judgment as a Christian. But that is exactly what the pastor had done. In that moment I began to wonder why some Christians were so quick to pass judgment on those who didn't conform to their rigid standards of proper Christian behavior.

Vernon never went to church with us, and neither did Elvis. I was a curious kid, and one time I blurted out, "Elvis, how come you don't go to church?"

He looked at me and smiled. "Well, Billy," he said, "I love going to church. And you know how much I read the Bible, right?"

"Yes."

"But I'm afraid if I go in, people will pay more attention to me than they would the preacher." Then Elvis explained the meaning of Matthew 18:20, where Jesus said, "For where two or three gather in my name, there am I with them." Elvis knew that being the church and worshiping with God's people didn't always have to take place in a church building.

He wasn't usually a morning person, but he watched a lot of gospel preachers on TV. There would be times when he would get up, especially on Sundays when he was in Memphis, and watch the gospel shows featuring different singers. He would just sit there and listen. Sometimes he would talk about going to church when he was growing up.

Elvis told me that after he and his family moved to Memphis in 1948, he would sometimes sneak out of the house and go to the Black churches to watch their gospel shows. One time he said to me, "Billy, when I first became famous, people thought I was the Antichrist because I moved around onstage."

"What do you mean?"

He explained, "The Holy Spirit touches these gospel singers and they can't stand still. They inspired me to move in the same way." Even some of the Black gospel churches in Memphis would see Elvis come in, and they would welcome him. He said, "I would stand there on the back row and watch the preachers. The Black preachers seem to know God better than most people. You can hear it in their voices. They've got a personal relationship with God."

Elvis had the same thing. I'll never forget him saying, "Me and God are close. We're so close. He knows me by my first name, and I know his name."

Because of my relationship with Elvis, and because I'm a Christian, people often ask me where I got my faith. That's where—I learned it from Elvis. It's one of the many gifts he gave me.

He talked to God. He would pray. He would sometimes sit in his room, closed off in silence, with nobody around. He would say, "Just talk to God like I'm talking to you right now." Elvis was always asking God for help or guidance. Sometimes he would sit in his room and talk to God out loud just like you would talk to another person. He even had the Serenity Prayer posted on the wall in his bedroom at Graceland.

People called Elvis "the King," but his response was, "No, there is only one true King. That's Jesus."

Even though I learned a lot from Elvis about faith, and I was involved in church as well, I still had questions. One time I went to his room to ask him a particularly confusing question. I said, "We have the Church of Christ, Methodist, Catholic, Baptist, and other denominations. Which one is correct?"

"What do you mean?"

I explained, "Well, they all say you've got to believe this way or that way, especially the Church of Christ." I had always been taught that if you didn't believe like Church of Christ folks, you would go to hell. "Which one should I believe?"

Elvis pointed to his Bible and said, "Everything you should believe is right there. Don't put labels on anything. That's where you get hung up. But as long as you believe that Jesus came and died for your sins, with all your heart and soul, that's all you need."

"Well, what about trying to be right or wrong?"

"If you believe what the Bible says, you'll *do* right." He also added, "Don't put your eyes on any man, even me. They all fall short. Nobody can live the perfect life. Put your faith in the Lord, and look to him."

∽

I had plenty of spiritual conversations with Elvis over the years. But those conversations happened in a setting of fun and family. When you feel loved and accepted, and you're having a lot of fun, you're much more open to spiritual teaching. Life at Graceland was no exception.

We were throwing the football in the front yard one day. Elvis was doing the throwing, while me, Rick, David, and some of the guys were the receivers. As I was lining up, Elvis yelled, "Go long, Billy!" That meant he wanted to throw a deep pass, so I took off as fast as I could run.

I was looking back as Elvis threw the ball. I watched as it arched in the air and made an adjustment in my route so the ball would land in my hands. I was thinking to myself, *Boy, this is going to look cool.*

Just as the ball was about to touch my hands, I saw a tree in the corner of my eye. The next thing I knew, I was lying on the ground, looking at the sky.

I didn't know you could see stars in daylight, but I saw them that day. I had run into the tree. As I lay there, I heard laughing and managed to raise up a little. I looked back, and there was Elvis, lying on the ground, laughing. Everyone else was bent over, holding their stomachs as they laughed.

I wanted to get up, but I was still reeling from the collision, so I lay back down. A couple of seconds later, Elvis was standing above me with a concerned look on his face. He asked, "Are you okay, Billy?"

"Yeah, I'm okay." As soon as I said that, he started laughing again. I could see tears were coming to his eyes. By now, everyone was standing around me, laughing. I lay there and eventually managed a smile because I knew it had to look funny, me running into a tree.

Elvis then asked, "Can you get up?"

I said, "Yeah, I think so." He reached his hand out to help me up. As I stood there, everyone asked if I was okay. I reassured them I was.

Then Elvis said, "I think that's enough football for today. Let's go inside."

As we walked toward the house, Elvis put his arm around my shoulders and said, "You really looked great, Billy. I thought you had it, and it would have been a great catch."

"Thanks, Elvis . . . but who put that tree in my way?"

He had to sit on the steps as he started laughing again. I stood there, looking at him and smiling, which made him laugh even harder. The tears came back and he begged me, "Please stop, Billy! Please!"

I was getting a kick out of seeing Elvis laughing and begging me to stop. So, I made it even funnier and said, "Are you okay, Elvis? You need any help getting up?" I put my hand out, as he had done. That made him laugh even more.

He begged harder now. "Please, Billy! Please stop!"

It took a few minutes for him to stop laughing. I even laughed a little myself. Finally, he got up and we walked into the house. As the day wore on, Elvis would ask if I was okay. I said I was; then he'd smile at me.

"You are one tough guy, Billy."

"Thanks, Elvis. I learned something today."

"What's that?"

"I'll never go long again. You can bet your money on that!"

That got him laughing all over again.

Elvis taught me that spiritual training has to happen in an atmosphere of love, acceptance, and good old-fashioned fun. We would often go outside to throw the football around with some of the guys. It was part of life at Graceland. He took the time to build a relationship with us so that we would be receptive to what he was teaching us.

∾

One of the reasons life at Graceland was so much fun is that Elvis was constantly giving gifts to people. He loved making others happy. However, he didn't like people making a fuss over *his* birthday.

One year, when we were a bit older, my brothers and I were determined to give Elvis something special for his birthday, on January 8. We looked at each other and said, "What do we give this guy? He's got everything in the world." We knew he loved cars, so we decided to build him some model cars. We each picked out a different car; then we put them together and painted them ourselves. They weren't professionally built, of course, but we did the best we could.

We wrapped the model cars in paper, placed them in shoeboxes, and stuffed paper around the cars so they wouldn't rattle around. Elvis was notorious for shaking gifts and trying to guess what was inside. We wanted it to be a surprise, so we did our best to keep it a mystery.

When Elvis was opening his gifts, he spotted ours and said, "Oh, I see these are from Billy, Ricky, and David. I wonder what they could be?" Sure enough, he shook the boxes, trying to figure out what was inside. When he opened the boxes, he seemed genuinely delighted. He hugged each of us and said, "Thank you, thank you, thank you!" He told everyone there, "These are the best presents I got this year!" You would have thought we had given him real cars from the look on his face and how happy he was.

After everyone left, he asked my brothers and me to follow him up to his room. He took the cars and placed them on his desk. We sat and talked for a little while.

As he was looking at the cars, tears came to his eyes. He asked us to come to where he was sitting, behind his desk. Then he hugged us again. He said, "You guys are the best birthday present I ever got."

We smiled at him and said, "Happy birthday, Elvis." He was the best gift anyone had given to *us*.

The gift of Elvis's presence was especially meaningful whenever he was absent. This was especially obvious when he was gone for longer periods of time for a movie shoot. During the 1960s, Elvis would shoot multiple movies per year, so every few months he would leave to do another one.

After each movie, Vernon would get a call from Elvis. He would tell him, "Daddy, we're leaving LA" and then what time he would get home. When we got the news, Graceland would fill with anticipation. We would all gather around to welcome him home.

Every time Elvis came home, it was a big deal. My brothers and I would usually miss school the next day because it would be late when he would arrive. All the employees, the wives, and girlfriends of the entourage would be there with us. The atmosphere was so thick with excitement, you could cut it with a knife.

We would usually get a call when Elvis and his entourage were in Arkansas, and someone would give us an estimated arrival time. Whoever took the call would tell us how many hours away they were. The excitement would rise even higher with each passing minute.

Then it happened. The guard at the gate would call the house and say, "They are pulling through the gates now." We would all run to the front door, walk out onto the steps, and watch the bus make its way to the front door.

When the bus came to a stop, the door would open. We would all start to applaud. That's how excited we were!

As Elvis stepped from the bus, he would exclaim, "It's great to be home!" Then he would make his way around the crowd, giving everyone a hug. He would also thank them for welcoming him home.

After he finished with everyone, Elvis would look for us boys. When he saw us, we'd run to him and he would kneel down and give us a hug. He would ask how we were doing and what we had been up to. After a couple of minutes, he would stand up, put David on his shoulders, and then Rick and I would grab his legs and hang on.

Even the house seemed to change when Elvis came home. It was full of life again. Elvis's presence was so strong, it seemed even to make the house glow. Homecomings at Graceland were always a big affair.

On that day when we became part of rock and roll's first family, I was introduced to a world people can only dream about. Once I did a little research on the world's population in 1960. It was about 3 billion people. Out of that 3 billion, only three would become Elvis Presley's stepbrothers.

At that time, we didn't know who Elvis was or what he did for a living. We were too young to care. But we knew he was special. There was something about him that drew us close to him. In our eyes, he was just like us, only bigger.

As I look back on that time, it's almost like a fairy tale, complete with a King and a castle. My life was a rock and roll version of Camelot. But I wasn't just one of the King's men. I was his brother.

THREE

YOU'LL NEVER
WALK ALONE

Most people who have older siblings go to them for advice. It was no different with us, except the person we went to was Elvis Presley. We asked him for advice about everything: life, love, girls, music, faith, career, you name it. I often call this my "Elvis education" because I learned so much from him.

When we would go to him for advice, he would always give us a loving, knowing smile, then say, "What is it, young one?" Then he would proceed to discuss whatever topic we brought to him. He always had time for us and never rushed through the discussion. After our talks, we'd walk away with a newfound sense of confidence or a fresh perspective.

Elvis took great pride in playing his newfound role as a big brother. At Graceland, the school of life was in session every day. Sometimes the lessons took place in the most unusual ways.

Many people don't know that Elvis loved cartoons. My brothers and I loved them, of course, but to our great surprise, he came to love them too. When he was home, it became our Wednesday night tradition to watch *The Bugs Bunny Show*. We'd take some chairs from the kitchen table and pull them closer to the TV.

Those special times were Elvis's way of bonding with us after the pressure of filming a movie. I remember a couple of times when someone would come up to us while we were watching TV. Elvis would either put his hand up to stop them or say, "It can wait until the show is over." Whenever that happened, my brothers and I would look at Elvis and smile. He would wink at us, and we'd continue watching our show.

He liked other TV shows from the 1960s as well. He loved *Star Trek* in particular. One time I asked him, "Why do you like it? It's kind of cheesy."

Elvis said, "Yeah, it's cheesy. Nothing wrong with a little cheese." Then he said, "I like it because of Spock."

I was surprised at his answer. "What do you like about Spock?"

"I like his sense of logic." Then he laughed.

As I look back on those first few years at Graceland, I realize that my brothers and I gave Elvis an excuse to be a kid again.

Vernon had a different perspective. He would say, "I'll be glad when you boys get a little older."

Elvis would counter with, "Let them be kids, Daddy. You only get to be a kid for a short amount of time." Elvis encouraged us to embrace the fun and innocence of childhood. He taught us the value of laughing, of having a sense of childlike wonder, of being with your family. In this setting of family and laughter, I learned to think bigger.

When we talked about my hopes and dreams, Elvis would say, "Always dream big, Billy. There's nothing in this world you can't do. The only thing holding anyone back is themselves. Go after your dreams and goals with everything you have in you. Don't listen to those that say you can't do this or that. People who say that are the ones who gave up on their hopes and dreams."

He continued by giving me advice about failure. "Don't worry about failing. If you don't accomplish what you set out to do, be proud that you gave it everything you had, that you left nothing to chance. Then and only then can you look back at what you did. Hopefully you learned an important life lesson—that your hopes and dreams don't always come true. But be thankful you had the chance to pursue them and came away being a stronger, better person for it."

Elvis made me feel like I could do anything.

∽

Even though me and my brothers loved getting our "Elvis education," our formal education was suffering a bit. We didn't do too well in school because the first couple of years at Graceland, Elvis would keep us out at night and we missed too much school. He would take us to the fair-grounds, the movies, or the roller-skating rink when he was home.

Elvis was a nocturnal creature to begin with. He would sometimes get up around one or two in the afternoon and stay up very late, depending on what was going on. Oftentimes, in the late afternoon, he would take us to a place around the corner to get a milkshake called the "Purple Cow." Elvis would say to the three of us, "Let's go get a Purple Cow!" and off we would go.

This didn't always sit well with our mother. Graceland was a bit like a party atmosphere, which was not conducive to keeping a school schedule for young boys. To resolve the situation, we had a family meeting and it was agreed that Vernon, my mother, and us boys would move into a separate house. Elvis bought a house on nearby Acacia Street, and Vernon traded it for one on Hermitage Street, where we moved in. People often think that we were asked to leave Graceland, which was not true. My mother wanted us to be in our own home environment. Elvis said, "I don't want you to go, but I understand."

While we lived in the house on Hermitage, Vernon was having a brand-new home built for us on nearby Dolan Street. One night, a few days after we had moved in, Elvis came over. It was around midnight. My brothers and I had already gone to bed. We slept in bunk beds stacked three high, which I always thought was cool.

We were sleeping, when suddenly Elvis came rushing into our room and woke us up. He was excited and said, "Hurry up and get dressed, boys! We're going to the fairgrounds."

He started throwing us our clothes and helping David get dressed since he was the youngest. David looked at Elvis and said, "I can do this myself. I'm a big boy now."

Elvis stopped and looked at him and smiled, then laughed and said, "Yes, you are, little man."

As we were leaving, Mom kept reminding Elvis that this was a school night and we couldn't do this all the time. She argued that it was important for us to get enough sleep so we could get an education at school. I'll never forget what Elvis said next. "There's more to life than learning from books, Dee. There's life experiences, and I want my boys to have both."

Elvis and my mother had occasional disagreements about activities that were appropriate for young boys. But just like the rest of the world, it was hard for her to resist Elvis's charm. He could be very persuasive.

∽

One of the most important ways for a young person to expand their mind is by learning music. And who better to teach us than the King of Rock and Roll himself? It seemed the one constant in my seventeen years with Elvis was music. My brothers and I were raised on rock, and Elvis taught us everything he knew about making it roll.

In the mid-1960s I had started a band with some friends. We got a little tape recorder and recorded "I'm a Believer" by the Monkees. I remember playing Elvis a demo of one of our sessions.

The guys in the band put me up to playing it for Elvis. They wanted to know what he thought. I, on the other hand, was a little hesitant. I knew it had to be good or Elvis wouldn't like it. It didn't take me long as a kid to become familiar with Elvis's musical taste. But the guys persisted, so I promised I'd play it for him.

One afternoon Elvis came over to the Dolan house to visit. He said, "I was walking around the barn and thought I'd stop in to say hello." Our house on Dolan Drive was right behind Graceland and just a stone's throw away from the barn.

Usually when he did this, he'd take some time to teach my brothers and me something new on our instruments. But this time I decided to play the tape for him. I asked, "Could I play a demo tape for you, Elvis?"

A big smile spread across his face. "Sure, Billy. Who is it?"

"Oh, I have a band. It's us playing." I hoped he would be proud.

Elvis's smile got even bigger when I said that. I went and got the tape recorder. When I came back, Elvis, Rick, and David were sitting in the den. Vernon and Mom were doing something but excused themselves.

Before I played the tape, I said, "Now, don't expect much, Elvis. This is only our third rehearsal." I was nervous and didn't want to hit play.

Elvis said, "Billy, don't be worried. I'm sure I'll like it. Just play the tape."

I said okay, pushed the play button, then sat back and watched Elvis. He looked at me the whole time the song played. He started tapping his foot to the beat. I was feeling a little better now.

Then we got to the end. The Monkees closed out that song with, "I'm a believer, yeah, yeah, yeah." We did it just like them. Elvis fought back a laugh, and I hung my head in disappointment.

He got up and walked over to me. He put his hand on my chin and pulled my head up. He said, "Billy, that was very good. In fact, I'm a little surprised at how good you've become on the bass. But the vocals at the end were a little weak."

"I really didn't want to play this for you, Elvis. I knew you wouldn't like it."

The smile on Elvis's face changed to a serious look now. I started to get scared. Then he said, "Billy, never put yourself down. Y'all did your best, and that's good enough for me. As I said, the music was good but the vocals need a little more work." Then he added, "Can I be a little honest here?"

I said, "Sure," and he asked me to play just the ending. After he heard it again, he asked me to stop it as we were going into the "Yeah, yeah, yeah" part. He said, "The next time you sing this part, let it come from your stomach, not your throat. Here: try it with me. Let's sing 'Yeah, yeah, yeah.'" I agreed.

Elvis put his hand on my stomach, then said, "Now sing it, Billy." We both sang it. When we finished, he said, "Pretty good, Billy, but push a little harder next time. Let's do it again."

We sang it again, and this time he said, "Much better, Billy. Now, one more time." We sang it yet again, and this time he said, "Now you're getting it, Billy!"

He continued, "The next time you and your band practice, show them what I just taught you. Then bring me the tape and play it for me."

"Okay, Elvis. I will."

He didn't only teach us about rock and roll. He was interested in all kinds of music. From the very beginning, Elvis mentored us as musicians and made it clear he had faith we could improve our craft.

The first Christmas we were at Graceland, my mom decided she wanted me to take piano lessons. The teacher would come to Graceland and we would have lessons in the piano room. One day I was walking by the room and heard Elvis playing "How Great Thou Art." He saw me walk by and said, "I understand you've been taking piano lessons. Can you show me what you know?"

I sat down beside him at the piano and went through the notes E, G, B, D, F for "every good boy does fine," the notes on the lines of treble clef.

He said, "It's kinda hard, huh?" Then he showed me a few exercises and we played "O Holy Night" together. He explained it was a song about the birth of Jesus. When we finished, he said, "Remember this: no one taught me how to play, and some people think I'm pretty good at it."

As I look back on it now, I see what he was doing. He was trying to plant seeds early in my life about the Lord through that hymn. He was also giving me a sense of confidence in my abilities, a feeling that I could do anything if I put my mind to it.

∞

Who was Elvis?

Everyone has a different answer to that question. He was, and still is, many things to many people. To millions of fans around the world, he remains the King of Rock and Roll, a force of nature that shook the world like a Cat 5 hurricane.

To me, Ricky, and David, he was our brother. But he was much more than that. Elvis became a father figure and the alpha male in our lives. He was a mentor and teacher who gave us a home, a safe and secure place to spread our wings and rise to our potential.

The wisdom I learned from Elvis about life and music was worth far more than any diploma or college degree could ever give me. He taught me not only how to make music, but how to make a life.

Proverbs 18:24 says, "One who has unreliable friends soon comes to ruin, but there is a friend who sticks closer than a brother." Elvis was the most reliable friend—and brother—anyone could ask for.

When we came into his life, he saw three young boys. He took on the responsibility of raising us as his own. Like an artist who examines a blank canvas, deciding what to paint, Elvis saw the potential inside those boys and began to work with us.

As I look back on those years—"The wonder years," as they are called—I'm grateful we had a man like Elvis to be our guide. He showed us a world where everything is possible and dreams really can come true.

FOUR

IN MY FATHER'S HOUSE

Even though Elvis fulfilled the roles of both a brother and father figure, there was only one "Daddy" at Graceland, and that was Vernon Presley. In fact, Elvis continued to call Vernon "Daddy" even as an adult. It was a term of affection. But it was also Elvis's way of recognizing that whatever level of success he might achieve, he would always still have a father who deserved respect. It took us a while, but we learned to call Vernon "Daddy" as well.

Coming from a military existence to a life with Elvis was a drastic change, to say the least. We loved having fourteen acres as our playground. Plus, we had all kinds of animals there, including chickens, peacocks, donkeys, and ducks.

We spent most of our days following Elvis's uncle Vester. He was the groundskeeper at that time. We helped him feed the animals, gather the eggs, and even mow the backyard.

In July 1960, a few months after we arrived at Graceland, Vernon and my mother told us they were going on a vacation. They said they would have a big surprise for us when they came back. After the surprise we got when we moved to Graceland, I didn't see how anything could get better than it already was. They also said Elvis and the staff would watch over us while they were gone.

This wasn't unusual because Elvis had become not only our big brother but our primary father figure as well. He took more of a role in our upbringing than Vernon did. While he and my mother were gone, Elvis took us to the fairgrounds several times, since it was summer.

When Vernon and Mom returned, they said we were going to have a family meeting. I didn't know what that meant, since I'd never been in a family meeting before. Then again, I'd never seen anything like Graceland before, so I knew it must be something good.

Vernon said, "When Elvis wakes up, we'll have the meeting." The three of us boys decided to go outside to play while we waited on Elvis.

After Elvis woke up and ate his breakfast, we were called inside and told to have a seat at the kitchen table. Vernon and Mom sat together while Elvis stood up and leaned over the counter. When we took our seats, the family meeting started.

Mom said, "Boys, I have some great news. Vernon and I got married while we were away."

Rick, David, and I looked at each other. We didn't know what to say. The room got quiet fast. We looked at Elvis, and he smiled at us.

David broke the silence. "What happened to Daddy?"

Mom said, "Things just didn't work out, son. Someday you'll understand."

Elvis could sense the confusion and fear that came over us. That's when he spoke up and said, "The great thing about this, boys, is that we're now officially brothers. We're going to be a big, happy family."

We still didn't know what was going on, but we liked the way Elvis was explaining things to us. The marriage was making official what we had already accepted in our hearts. We looked at Vernon, then looked back at Elvis. He had this big smile on his face. He said, "Now you don't have to say 'Mr. Presley' anymore. Now he's 'Daddy.'"

Then Elvis turned to Vernon and said, "Ain't that right, Daddy?"

"That's right, son."

Vernon was smiling at us the whole time. Then he said, "Come here, boys." We got up from our seats and walked over to him. We stood in front of him. He said, "I promise to take care of you just like you were my own."

Elvis could see we were still confused. To help ease the mood, he said, "Oh no! You're in for it now, boys!" Then he broke out laughing. We turned to Elvis and began to smile.

Then Elvis said something that I'll never forget. "I promise, boys, I'll always be here for you. I'll take care of you."

It took a while for us to get used to calling Vernon "Daddy." If one of us called him "Mr. Presley" and Elvis was around, he would say, "What did you say?"

"I'm sorry. I mean 'Daddy.'"

Elvis would give us that big smile and say, "That's better, boys."

That is how Vernon went from "Mr. Presley" to "Daddy" in just a few minutes. To most people, this probably seems like an abrupt change from our former life. But none of us boys were close to our birth father. He had never been an active part of our lives. We were thrilled to finally have not only one, but two male figures who took an interest in our lives and wanted us to be a part of their family.

As our new daddy, Vernon taught us surprising life lessons I still remember today. Some of these were lessons he had taught Elvis, and now we were learning them as well.

On several occasions, Rick, David, and I were sent home from school for fighting. This only happened at Graceland Elementary. When we got older, everyone pretty much left us alone. But in the early years it was different.

There were two reasons for the fights, which we never started. The first reason was that it seemed like some guys thought they'd impress the students at school if they beat up Elvis's little brothers. The second reason was that if my brothers and I saw a kid being bullied, we'd always step in if they couldn't defend themselves.

Every time we were sent home, it was Vernon who came and picked us up. Now, I'll admit, when he came to get me, I was scared. I knew Vernon didn't put up with us being disobedient. He was a firm believer in "spare the rod, spoil the child."

This is how things normally went: When he came to pick us up, he would ask, "What happened?" I knew I had better talk fast if I didn't want to get my behind whipped. So, I'd tell him what happened.

When I did, something unexpected would happen. He would say, "You know, Elvis had the same problem in school."

"Really? Why would anyone want to pick on Elvis?"

"A lot of the guys at school didn't like Elvis because he looked different. They thought if they beat him up, it would make them look tough."

"Did Elvis get sent home from school too?"

"Oh yeah."

Usually after something like this happened, Vernon would tell us more stories about Elvis and his school years. He usually did this when we were watching "The Late Show," a Memphis TV program that played movies late at night. This was often the time when we would sit and relax, just hearing Vernon's stories. He would tell us the struggles Elvis had as a young man in school. It helped me understand that it's okay to be different.

Elvis was a very sensitive man. He didn't like to fight, but he would if he was backed into a corner. Plus, he loved everyone and could never figure out why anyone would want to harm him. It also baffled him why someone would want to pick on his new younger brothers just because they had a different last name.

As a first grader, I was teased by older kids as they hurled this joke at me: "Why did little Johnny put his brother under the stairs? Because he wanted a stepbrother."

One day Elvis picked me up from school and I repeated the joke to him. He stopped the car as if I had said a bad word. It scared me.

He said, "Where'd you hear that?"

"Hear what?"

"Stepbrother."

"From the kids at school. That's what they're saying."

Elvis got a little angry. "I don't care what any of the kids said. You're my *brother*. You always will be."

The conversation didn't stop with Vernon. He always told Elvis what had happened. If Elvis was home, he'd talk to me, Rick, and David about school and fighting. If he was away, making a movie, then he'd talk to us when he came home. In fact, Vernon told Elvis everything we did when we were growing up. It always surprised us that when Elvis came home from making a movie, he would talk about something only Vernon or Mom would know that had happened while he was gone.

From the very beginning of our life at Graceland, Vernon instilled in us the importance of family. "Family is everything," he would say. "Without family, you have nothing."

Despite all the luxury and trappings of success at Graceland, we had what matters most: a loving family. We were blessed not only to have Elvis as the best older brother a boy could ask for, but also a stepfather who embraced us as his own kids. We were wealthy in the way Proverbs 1:8–9 describes:

> Listen, my son, to your father's instruction
> and do not forsake your mother's teaching.
> They are a garland to grace your head
> and a chain to adorn your neck.

If wisdom and instruction could be turned into gold, we were the richest kids in Memphis.

⚬⚬

Elvis was a household icon by the time my brothers and I moved into Graceland. He may have been the King, but he was still Vernon's son.

Vernon didn't have any say in creative decisions related to Elvis's career, but he was very involved in the day-to-day affairs of Graceland. He never said, "You should record this certain song" or "You ought to star in this certain movie." Instead, Vernon handled Elvis's personal business and running the estate.

Elvis was famously known for having a huge car collection, and it was one of the few things they ever argued about. Vernon would say, "Elvis, you're going to drive us to the poorhouse with these cars."

But Elvis would laugh and say, "Well, at least we'll be going there in a new car." He was quick-witted like that. Or he would try to reason with Vernon and say, "I'll just go and make another movie or do another concert tour. Don't worry about it, Daddy. You can't take it with you."

Money was not a big issue to Elvis. It wasn't what made his world go round. But Vernon was different. He knew the value of a dollar. He remembered those days of having nothing probably better than Elvis did. That's why he was very tight with money.

I didn't hear Elvis and Vernon argue very often, but when I did, I knew it was a big deal. The first time I saw anything like this was after Vernon and my mom were married. My brothers and I were playing in the backyard.

Vernon came out into the yard and said, "Okay, boys, keep on playing out here. I'll be right back." We weren't that far away and could hear him and Elvis arguing. Elvis said, "Daddy, I don't care what it takes. I want this!"

I found out later that Elvis had been talking to our birth father because he wanted to get our names changed to Presley so we could be his brothers not only by marriage, but in name as well. But my father refused and said, "You've taken my boys. You can't take their name too." That wasn't true, because nobody "took" us away. He had ceased being a father figure long before my mother married Vernon. Nevertheless, Elvis respected my father's decision and backed off.

Later that day, Elvis came to us boys. He said, "I know you heard me and Daddy getting into it earlier. I just wanted you to know I was trying to get your last name changed." He didn't like the idea of us seeing him get mad and wanted to explain what was going on.

It was the only battle I ever saw him lose.

Even though I have always carried my birth father's last name, I only saw him three more times after we moved to Graceland. The first time was when he came to Memphis for a few days when he and my mom were finalizing their divorce. As he was leaving, he picked me up and said, "Always watch after your mom." The second time was when I went to visit him as an adult many years later. The third time was before he passed away in 1991.

There could not have been a greater contrast between him and Elvis. My birth father was cold, distant, and pushed people away. Elvis, on the other hand, was warm, inviting, and welcomed us into his family. He loved to let people know, "These are my boys. You better not touch them."

It all began with Vernon, the original Presley man, who loved and supported Elvis just as Elvis did the same for us. That's why I think of Vernon as my father and my biological father, Bill, as my birth father.

Years later, when I became a father myself, I tried to put into practice all I had learned from Elvis as well as Vernon. I vowed that if I ever had kids, they would know their father. I didn't have a close relationship with my birth father and didn't want my own kids to have that same experience. Thankfully, I had two wonderful father figures growing up who showed me the way.

FIVE

SOMEBODY BIGGER THAN YOU AND I

As my brothers and I got to know Elvis in the 1960s, we started to gradually understand how famous he was. When you live with someone day in and day out, when you eat meals with him and play with him, it's hard to grasp how the rest of the world feels about him. I remember the first time I caught a glimpse of Elvis's fame.

During our first year at Graceland, when I was in the first grade, Vernon would take me to school in the pink Cadillac. He told me to always look for that car after school.

One day I was walking out to the car and noticed a lot of kids standing around it and wondered what was going on. As I got closer, I noticed Elvis was driving. My brothers and I didn't know who Elvis was when we moved to Graceland, nor did we know what he did for a living. We had never seen any of his movies or heard any of his records. At first, he was just a cool guy who loved to have fun and give presents to everyone.

When I got in the car, Elvis said, "Hi, Billy. How was school?"

I looked at the crowd around the car and said, "It was okay, Elvis. What are you doing?"

"I thought I'd pick you up today. I'm just signing some autographs."

"Autographs? What's that?"

Elvis smiled. "You write your name on some paper for someone. It's called an autograph."

I was still looking at all the kids. Now some of the teachers and parents were gathering around the car. I didn't know why and said, "Okay."

Elvis asked everyone, "Would you like to have my little brother's autograph?" All the girls squealed and said yes. Everyone started sticking their hands in the car, shoving pieces of paper at Elvis. He smiled at me again and said, "It's okay, Billy. Just write your name on it." So, I reached into my book bag, took out a red crayon, and started writing "Billy" on them.

After a few minutes, Elvis told everyone we needed to leave. But before we drove away, Elvis said, "Would some of you older kids please keep an eye on my little brother? He's new here and doesn't know anyone yet."

Again, all the girls squealed and shouted, "Yes, Elvis! We'll do anything for you!" Elvis smiled at the kids and thanked them. A couple of the older girls said, "If you ever need a babysitter, let us know."

Elvis laughed. "I'll do that."

As we drove away, I was thinking about what had just happened and said, "Are you famous?"

"Some people think I am."

"Are you more famous than Mickey Mouse?" That was the only famous person I knew at that time.

Elvis burst out laughing. Again, he said, "Some people think I am."

I looked at him, trying to think of something else to say. Elvis sensed that I was confused. He reached over and pulled me next to him as we drove to Graceland. He said, "Someday I'll get Daddy to show you some of my movies and play some of my records for you, Billy."

I was only seven years old and didn't think much about it, so I said, "That would be neat, Elvis."

Thus began our long and slow education into Elvis's world, with the man himself as our guide and instructor.

Over the next few years, we sat in the basement at Graceland and watched Elvis's movies and listened to his records. We still didn't realize how big a star he was. When I would ask him about it, he would always downplay what he did. He would say, "My job isn't that important. I'm just an entertainer. What my fans and other people do for a living is more important than what I do."

My brothers and I never saw him the way fans do. We saw him as our brother. However, we got a firsthand glimpse into Elvis's world on February 25, 1961—our first concert.

This wasn't just any concert. It was Elvis's return to the stage in Memphis. I remember what Elvis told us before we went to the show. He said, "You boys are going to see something different tonight. I know you'll like it."

Vernon and Mom tried to explain what we were about to see on our way to Ellis Auditorium. None of what they said made any sense to us. I was eight, Ricky was seven, and David was five. We had never seen a concert before, nor did we know what a concert was. But we were excited because of what Elvis had said to us.

As we took our seats in the balcony of the left side of the stage, we noticed a lot of people. My brothers and I didn't sit down. Instead, we stood at the railing and looked down at everyone.

Suddenly the lights went down and people began to scream. That scared us, so we looked back at Mom and Vernon. They gave us a look that said everything was okay.

We turned around just as Elvis walked onstage. The crowd went crazy and the screaming became a roar. People were jumping up and down. Some rushed the stage as Elvis started singing. My brothers and

I looked at each other. We were confused. If everyone was having fun, why were they acting like this?

As the show went on, I noticed that my brothers and I were moving to the music. Elvis was right—we liked it! I even turned around once to see what Mom and Vernon were doing. They were smiling and clapping their hands. They winked at me, which reassured me that everything was all right.

After the show, we went back to Graceland and waited for Elvis to arrive. The house was full of friends and family. When Elvis got home, everyone congratulated him. He saw my brothers and me standing off to the side and walked over to us, knelt down, then asked, "What did you boys think of that?"

All three of us said, "We liked it. It was cool. It was neat." Then I asked, "Why was everyone screaming and yelling?"

Elvis smiled. "That's what some people do when they like something."

David said, "A lot of people must like you, because everyone was yelling and screaming." Rick agreed. Elvis smiled at us and gave us a hug. Then he said, "This is just the beginning, boys."

He was right. It wasn't until eight years later, in 1969, that I fully grasped how important Elvis was to so many people.

I'd had my heart set on going to Woodstock, but the family had planned a vacation in Vegas because Elvis was opening his act there. I went to the concert, but my heart wasn't in it. I assumed I was going to see a bunch of people older than me. While I loved Elvis as my brother, his music skewed a bit older than my generation, which loved the Beatles.

But when I sat down at the concert, I noticed all these celebrities, young and old people, a mixture of every kind of person you could imagine. When Elvis came out and did the show, I think I took one breath and sat there with my jaw hitting the floor. I was blown away by Elvis's energy and the crowd's excitement. I felt as if I was seeing Elvis for the very first time.

After nine years of living with him, I thought, *Wow! Where has he been?* I had never seen that side of him before. That's when I finally understood why people called him the King.

When you're the King, the list of people who want to visit your castle is long . . . including the most famous band in the world.

∾

On August 19, 1966, the Beatles played a concert in Memphis. That was also the day they stopped by our house.

The Beatles had met Elvis a year earlier when they held a secret jam session in LA. He was one of their musical idols. Now that they were in town, they wanted to say hello to Elvis and have their picture taken in front of Graceland. However, Elvis was not home at the time, so they came to our house on nearby Dolan Street to get Vernon's permission.

It was around dinnertime when I heard a knock. Since I was the oldest, I jumped up to answer it. When I opened the door, a man was standing there. He introduced himself with an English accent. "Hello. My name is Brian Epstein. I'm the road manager of the Beatles. Is Mr. Presley here?"

I leaned to the right to look past him and saw a limo with the four Beatles sitting there. I said, "Yes, sir. Let me get him for you." I slowly closed the door, then ran to the living room, yelling, "The Beatles are here! The Beatles are here!"

Unfortunately, that was as close as I ever came to meeting the Beatles. My mom wouldn't let us go outside to meet them because of John Lennon's comment in the media that the Beatles were more popular than Jesus.

Elvis once told me the Beatles asked him, "How do you do it? The pressure is unbelievable. There's four of us, and that helps relieve some of the pressure. But there's only one of you."

Elvis didn't answer. He just sat back and smiled.

One time I heard Elvis say, "It's lonely at the top, but I love that lonesome feeling." The first time I heard that, I thought it was odd and didn't think about it. I just took it as him being funny. But as I got older, I began to understand what Elvis meant.

Why was it lonely for Elvis at the top? Because he had no peers in the entertainment world. There were lots of other singers, but none of them had accomplished what Elvis had, so he couldn't even ask any other entertainer what it was like to be a superstar. He was a superstar before the term was invented. Even John Lennon famously said, "Before Elvis, there was nothing."

How did Elvis do it? How did he stay grounded in his life and faith while also being the world's biggest entertainer?

One thing to keep in mind is that Elvis's temptations were far greater than almost any other human before him. He was a worldwide sensation who was adored by millions. I always say that he had the devil on one shoulder and God on the other. His head was stuck in the middle, constantly pulled in both directions.

But because of where he'd come from and his faith in God, he stayed grounded and humble. He wasn't perfect by any means. He pointed to Jesus as the only perfect person to have walked this earth.

Elvis knew who he was. He knew he was immensely gifted, and he knew where he stood in the music and entertainment world. But he didn't let it go to his head.

More than any other person I've ever known, Elvis lived out the words of 1 Peter 5:6–7. It says, "Humble yourselves, therefore, under God's mighty hand, that he may lift you up in due time. Cast all your anxiety on him because he cares for you."

Elvis had every right to claim his place among the royalty of music. He broke new ground and single-handedly built the template for what it means to be a rock and roll star. In the process, he changed the whole entertainment industry. Yet one of the first lessons Elvis taught me was, "Billy, it's just a job. We're no different, no better than anybody else. We entertain the common, everyday workers who make the world go round."

When people asked Elvis's political views, he would say, "I'm just an entertainer. I leave my political views out of it." He didn't think it was important, and he didn't believe in using celebrity status to influence anybody's way of thinking.

Elvis didn't get caught up in the head games and ego trips that consume so many celebrities. He was the exact same person onstage and off. He was the most grounded and confident person I've ever known, and he knew the secret for finding your place in this world.

One day, as a teenager, I went to Elvis and told him I didn't know what crowd I fit into.

He said, "In essence, what you're trying to do is find out who the real Billy is, correct?"

"Yeah."

"Remember, Billy, the mind is the devil's playground. Everybody knows the master of confusion is the devil. The mind believes it is the strongest organ. But the heart is God's playground. The heart is what keeps you going. It's actually the strongest organ."

I wasn't following him.

Elvis continued, "When you go to look for yourself, where are you going to look?"

I thought for a moment. "I don't know."

"Have you thought about the Bible? There are a lot of interesting characters in there. Read it and it will help you find who you are."

Elvis had a way of focusing on the essentials. No matter the situation—and no matter what season of the year—he could bring everything back to the simple truths of God.

SIX

I'LL BE HOME FOR CHRISTMAS

G rowing up at Graceland, I always looked forward to Christmas. The
Presley family went all out to decorate, gather friends and family,
and create holiday memories. But even with Elvis's fame and access to
anything he wanted, the focus wasn't just on decorations and gifts. He
also made sure we learned about the real meaning of Christmas: the gift
of Jesus and the hope we have in him.

There's a reason it's called "the good news"—it's news that will change
your life! But some people have still never heard it. That was the case
with my brothers and me. We weren't familiar with the Christmas story
when we moved into Graceland. We had never been active in a church. I
thought Christmas was all about getting toys.

But as soon as we began our first holiday season, Elvis started teaching us the meaning of Christmas. He would take us aside and say, "Boys,
it's not about presents. It's about Jesus's birthday. Let's not forget what
this day represents." As we would come to discover as we got older, we

had plenty of reasons to be grateful, since the holiday season at Graceland kicked off with Thanksgiving.

If Elvis was home, a typical Thanksgiving Day began with family and friends arriving at Graceland around noon. We would be all dressed up while the smell of turkey, ham, green beans, mashed potatoes, and pumpkin pie filled the house.

The guys would usually go to the den and watch a little bit of the parade, then football, on TV. In reality, we didn't watch much because we would all be joking around. The conversation always ended with how good the food smelled.

By 6:00 or 7:00 p.m., we would be sitting at the dinner table. After we all sat down, Elvis would ask everyone to tell what they were thankful for. It would start on his left and go around the table, ending with Elvis telling us what he was thankful for. He always said, "I'm thankful for my family, my friends, and my fans." After that, he would ask my mom to say a prayer. Then we would eat.

The conversation was always light and funny. Sometimes I thought Elvis and Vernon were competing on who could tell the most amusing stories. They would have everyone laughing as we enjoyed the meal.

After eating, everyone would thank Elvis for having them there at Graceland. He would say, "You made it special for all of us by being here." Someone would mention that Christmas was just around the corner, and that's when we would start making plans and looking forward to putting up the tree.

Decorating the tree was an event for family and friends at Graceland. One of the people who loved decorating the most was Priscilla Beaulieu. Her father was in the Air Force, and Elvis had met her while stationed in

Germany. He liked her immediately, and she moved to Memphis in 1963 to be closer to Elvis. They married in 1967.

A week or two before Christmas, Vernon would buy a real tree. The next day we would all get together to help put it up. We would have dinner first, then gather to place it in a stand that slowly rotated the tree as Christmas music played. The tree always stood in the dining room.

After that, we would hang lights on the tree. When these were in place, we would turn the stand to get a better view and adjust it if needed. Then we would hang the ornaments. Everyone would be joking and laughing as we worked.

Then came the tinsel. Priscilla liked to place it on the tree a couple of strands at a time. However, Elvis liked to throw handfuls of it at a time as he walked around the tree. It was hilarious listening to Priscilla say, "You're doing it wrong. It's supposed to be placed a few strands at a time."

Elvis would reply, "No, *you've* got it wrong" as everyone laughed. My brothers and I always followed Elvis's lead and threw tinsel everywhere. Priscilla would come behind us and try to remove what we had done, but she always gave up.

After we had finished with the tree, Elvis would place the star on top. Then we would plug in the tree, stand back, and admire what we had done. It was such a beautiful sight to see the lights come on and hear the music. You could feel the love in the room as we looked at one another and smiled.

But something strange always seemed to happen later that night. When we saw the tree the next day, a lot of the tinsel would have disappeared. With a hint of mischief in his eyes, Elvis would say, "I guess the tinsel fairy came last night and removed some of it."

Elvis loved to have fun and was like a big kid during Christmas. Shopping was no exception. When I was a little older, I was invited to help. He would have a store opened up after hours, and we would all get into our cars and follow him there. Once we were inside, Elvis would walk down each aisle and pick out something for everyone. He would hold up something and ask, "What do you think she would think of this?" or "Do you think he would like this?"

Elvis personally picked every present himself. If he held up a shirt or a jacket, he would say, "You know, this would look good on so-and-so." Then he might change his mind, smile, and jokingly say, "No, I think I'll get this for myself." His Christmas shopping sprees were all about showing love and generosity to his family and friends. Of course, those who helped him shop for gifts never knew what we were receiving because he would shop for those gifts separately.

After a few hours of shopping, he would have the gifts wrapped and we would load them into the cars. Back at Graceland, Elvis would arrange the presents under the tree.

We always had a formal affair on Christmas Eve. It started around 5:00 p.m., when all the family, friends, and employees would arrive. As soon as you walked in the door, you could smell the food cooking in the kitchen. The scents of turkey, ham, mashed potatoes, cornbread dressing, pumpkin pie, and much more filled the air. The maids, who worked full-time at Graceland, worked extra hard to prepare a feast like no other for Elvis and his friends and family.

There were appetizers laid out on the table for everyone to enjoy. Vernon particularly liked rum balls. He always seemed to get happier after eating a few! There was also live music, with a man walking around playing accordion as drinks were served. Everyone would stand around, talking and joking with each other, sharing funny things that happened during the year.

About thirty minutes after everyone had arrived, Elvis would make his entrance. I always thought he looked so cool, walking down the front stairway, smiling at everyone there. When he got to the main floor, he would walk up to every person, hug them, and thank them for being there.

After an hour or so, dinner would be served. Elvis led us in prayer, and then we would dig in. The conversation at the table was light and funny. When we were young, sometimes Elvis would ask me and my brothers, "Have y'all been good this year?" Of course, we always said yes. Then he would say, "Santa told me you were. Me and him are pretty tight, you know." Everyone would laugh at that.

After dinner we would open presents. The tradition never changed. First, Elvis would hand out his gifts to everyone. It was fun watching him dig for presents under the tree, because there were so many of them. His greatest joy was watching everyone open their gifts from him.

One time Elvis wanted to play a little joke on everyone. He handed out envelopes, and everyone looked at each other, wondering what it could be, then opened them at the same time. The surprised look on their faces was hilarious. Elvis had given everyone McDonald's gift cards! It didn't seem to go over too well, so that was the last time he did it.

As I got older, I began to watch Elvis a little more closely when he handed out gifts. The look on his face was priceless, and I could see the love he had for everyone. It was so strong you could feel it. Elvis was happiest during these times because he was a giver, not a taker.

Watching Elvis tear into his presents was like watching a child. Sometimes he would look up and see how everyone was watching him, and then he would try to act a little more grown-up. But after a few minutes, he would go right back to acting like a kid again.

After all the gifts were opened, we would show off what we had received. Elvis in particular made you think your gift to him was the greatest thing he had ever received.

As the celebration wound down, we would congratulate each other on our gifts. Elvis would say, "It's been a great year, but I know next year will be even better." Then we would end the day, basking in the loving spirit of Christmas with family and friends.

We had lots of fun with gifts, but Christmas with Elvis was never focused on just the material things. It was about gifts—the gift of friends, the gift of family, and the gift of faith.

My brothers and I shared an inside joke over the years: "The only difference between Christmas and any other day with Elvis was that we had a tree at Christmas." I'll never forget the way Elvis made other people feel like he truly appreciated them. However, Elvis's love for people at Christmas went far beyond his family. Oftentimes, he would help strangers who were in need.

One night we were sitting around Graceland, about a week before Christmas. Sonny West, one of Elvis's bodyguards, came and told him about a lady who had just lost everything she had in a fire. This deeply moved Elvis, who immediately said, "I'll help her."

It was a little late that night, so my brothers and I had to go home. I wasn't there when Elvis went into action, but the next day we were there when Elvis gave Sonny instructions on what to say if the lady asked who had done this. Elvis said, "Tell her Santa Claus did it."

I never asked Elvis what he did for the lady and didn't find out until 1988. I met the lady and had seen her at Graceland a couple of times in the 1960s. She was a friend of Sonny's. When we met, we had a talk and she told me what Elvis had done for her and her children.

She said Elvis had a store opened up and he bought clothes, furniture, and toys for her and her children. The next day he had someone rent an apartment, then had everything delivered there. Then he had Sonny pick her up and take her to her new apartment. She and her children were overjoyed and couldn't believe what they saw.

Before Sonny left, she said, "Tell Elvis I said thank you."

He smiled. "Santa Claus did this, not Elvis."

Her eyes filled with tears as she gave Sonny a hug. She said, "Then tell Santa Claus I said thank you. And tell Elvis thank you also."

They both laughed.

Some of Elvis's acts of love during the holidays were more public. Every year, Elvis enjoyed riding around Memphis and looking at the Christmas lights. One year he got an idea of riding around on motorcycles to look at the lights and do some Christmas caroling. We all put on our warmest clothing and rode around Memphis, stopping at various houses to sing a Christmas carol or two.

We didn't know any of the people when we stopped, but it was great to see the looks on their faces when they saw it was Elvis leading the choir! The Memphis press heard about it and dubbed us "El's Angels."

Christmas was so special to Elvis not just because of the fun or the presents, but for what it represents. He often talked about the birthday of Jesus. When I was growing up, he would tell me, "Just think, Billy. Jesus was born with nothing. His family was worse than poor, but look what he became."

Sometimes a tear would come to his eye when he talked about that special day. I remember one time when he said, "I so much want to be like Jesus."

I said, "You are, Elvis. You bring happiness, love, and joy to people's lives. You love to give to those in need." He smiled, gave me a hug, and thanked me for what I'd said.

Titus 3:4–5 says, "But when the kindness and love of God our Savior appeared, he saved us, not because of righteous things we had done, but because of his mercy." Kindness, love, and mercy. The best gift anyone could ever receive is also the gift God gave to us when Jesus was born. Because of his birth, death, and resurrection, we have hope.

Thank you, Elvis, for introducing me to the greatest gift of all.

SEVEN

IT IS NO SECRET
(WHAT GOD CAN DO)

I get questions and comments about Elvis every day. People ask me what it was like to grow up with him. They want to hear behind-the-scenes stories of life on the road. But most of all, they talk to me about the music.

After all, Elvis was *all about the music*. He was never far from music even when he was starring in big Hollywood films.

Whether it was singing gospel songs in front of a big audience or jamming with the boys, Elvis brought love and energy to his music. Near Psalm 137 in his Bible, he wrote, "The highest graces of music flow from the feelings of the heart-soul." I've never seen anyone live out this idea more than Elvis. He was a vessel of grace and energy God used to impact people in a way the world will never see again.

Elvis's favorite way to channel this energy was to sing gospel. Many people don't know that the only Grammy Awards Elvis won were for his gospel music. He had fun recording and performing rock and roll songs, like "Hound Dog," "Jailhouse Rock," "Suspicious Minds," and dozens of others, but Elvis's heart and soul were always with gospel music.

But it went beyond *his* heart and soul. Elvis's gospel music was so powerful it touched other people's hearts to the point where it changed their eternity.

I used to be a Harley salesman. In 2010, I was working in a Harley shop when I had a customer who was getting his bike customized and I wanted to check on it. I walked in the back, where the mechanics were, and as I was talking to one of the mechanics, a guy came up to me out of the blue and said, "You got a minute?"

I said yes. He continued, "You know, I never really cared for Elvis."

I thought, *Great. This guy has gone out of his way to give me a piece of his mind about Elvis.* But I listened.

He said, "I didn't really care for all the rock and roll stuff he did. But I've gotta tell you, I believe in the Lord because of the way he sang the gospel."

That took me by surprise. Bikers are not known for being softies. But here was this big old burly biker telling me how Elvis had changed his life. I said, "Thank you."

He said, "No, thank *you*, bro."

Most people who talk to me about Elvis will share that they loved this or that song, but I rarely hear people talk about his gospel music. It's funny that Elvis's rock and roll music received almost all the attention, yet it was gospel music that was closest to his heart. Elvis saw it as more than a performance. To him, it was a calling and a ministry.

It's not only that you can hear it in his voice when he sings songs about faith. You could also see it directly in Elvis's Bible. He often underlined verses that were important to him or made notes in the margins. For example, he wrote "Sing the Lord's praises" underneath Psalm 81 and "Sing for the glory of God" at the end of Psalms.

Elvis saw himself as a gospel singer who just happened to sing rock and roll and star in movies.

∾

Elvis may have had humble beginnings, but he blossomed into a highly skilled artist. He constantly worked to hone and perfect his craft. He was such a perfectionist that he would never listen to anything he recorded. One time I asked him, "Elvis, how come you don't listen to your own stuff?"

He said, "Billy, I know I can always go back and do it better. When I hear my own music, all I want to do is go fix it. But I can't, because it's already been done. So that's why I don't listen to my own stuff."

One time, he told me a funny little story about a producer. Elvis was in the booth, singing. The producer stopped him and said, "Why don't you sing it like this?" as he sang a couple of words.

Elvis looked at him through the glass window and said, "Why don't you come in here and sing it any way you want and I'll produce *you*?"

The producer just smiled and said, "Never mind. I guess I forgot who I was talking to." Nobody could tell Elvis what to do. He had a clear idea how he wanted to use his gift.

Elvis was a unique performer because he always sang other people's songs. He recorded hundreds of songs in his lifetime, but he was not much of a songwriter. He wrote one song in the 1950s, but that was about it. Elvis preferred to have other people write a great song, give it to him on a 45 record, and he would listen to it for twenty-four hours. Then he would find a way to channel his energy into that song and perform it in his unique way.

One day I walked into the den at Graceland, where Elvis was listening to a song by himself. I asked what he has doing. He said, "I'm just listening to a demo. I call it living with the song. When I'm thinking about recording a song, I play it over and over and over again until I get it in my head and make it my own."

This was true even with other artists' songs that he covered. Take Simon & Garfunkel's "Bridge Over Troubled Water." When Elvis sang it, the song became something completely different. Someone once told me that when Paul Simon heard Elvis perform that song at Madison Square Garden, he said, "That's the way the song should have been done." Elvis got the feeling of the song and made the sound and the arrangement unique to fit him.

The same is true with "Yesterday" by the Beatles. If you listen to their version and then listen to Elvis's version, there is a distinct difference. It's not that Elvis's version is better; it's just more soulful. He took the song and made it his own.

☙

If you were to open Elvis's Bible to the book of Ecclesiastes, you would see this written at the top of the page: "With the Holy Spirit one can moutains." He may have forgotten to write "move" before "mountains" and also misspelled "mountains," but the message is still the same.

The Holy Spirit indeed used Elvis to move mountains. He knew his voice was a gift from God. He reasoned that if his voice was a gift, he should use it in a way that God would want by singing gospel songs. That was his ministry.

Elvis was a firm believer in being in the Spirit. He loved the Holy Ghost. He would say, "It's the best feeling in the world when it overcomes you. You can do anything. You feel like you can climb the Empire State Building when the Holy Spirit fills you."

He would usually feel this way when he was talking about the Bible or singing gospel music. There were times I heard him pray and ask for God's wisdom and strength, and to fill him with his Holy Spirit.

Those were the three things he asked for often. More than once I heard him pray, "God, fill me with your Holy Spirit." The Spirit would come on when he was singing a gospel song and would get into it.

You could see it. He would go from just singing to suddenly being filled with the Spirit. He would start moving, and it was plain as day that something was stirring within him. He was in tune with God.

Elvis always prayed before he went onstage. Once I asked him why he did this. He replied, "Let me put it to you like this: Each show is different. It's like a first date. You never really know how the date will turn out, but you always hope it will be a good one. I want to make sure God blesses this show."

He prayed for everything. Maybe that is why there was a special kind of energy that seemed to surround Elvis. The charismatic character you saw in the movies or in concerts was not any different from the real-life Elvis offstage. He was the same.

You could literally feel his energy. He is the only person I've ever known who had that kind of power. I would be sitting there watching TV or having dinner in the basement, and all of a sudden, I'd just feel it. I would turn around, and there stood Elvis. His presence was that strong.

Somehow, he was a vessel of energy God used to impact people. I've never seen anything like it. That's what made his music so powerful.

∞

More than anything, Elvis wanted to honor God with his talent. He knew it was a gift and treated it that way. That's why he wanted to be excellent in everything he did.

Elvis never did anything halfway. It was all or nothing with him, especially with music. Over the years, people have remarked that he could sing the phone book and it would have been great. It's true because he put his heart and soul into it.

It was the same when Elvis wanted to play or just have fun. He put everything he had into each one. He often told me, "Billy, always try to be the best at whatever you do. Be the best at your job, and be the best when you play."

When he first told me this, I asked, "But what if I'm not the best, Elvis?"

He said, "Then at least you have peace of mind knowing you put everything into it. You left nothing on the table. And you can truthfully say you gave it your best shot. That in itself is satisfying." Then he added a little piece of wisdom. "But just because you didn't succeed the first time, never give up. Try, try, try again."

Many people have seen at least one of Elvis's movies. Who else could have starred in those silly movies and been successful at it? No one. He didn't really care for them, but he still put everything he had into each one. And it worked. Even the soundtracks to the movies were creative and fun.

Elvis knew God had given him a great talent. He knew where his talent came from. He would sometimes ask, "Why me, Lord? Why did you pick me for this assignment?" He asked God that question a lot, but he didn't feel it was a burden to be the Elvis people knew and loved. What he meant was, "Why, God, did you bless me with these gifts?"

Everybody knew Elvis was uniquely blessed. Simply by being around him all the time, my brothers and I were drawn to music also. We hoped we might be able to harness some of the musical power.

One day, after we had moved to the house on Dolan Street, my brother David and I were jamming in the shed by the pool. David was on drums and I was playing bass. We had Led Zeppelin cranked up on the stereo, and we were playing along with the record.

Suddenly the door flew open and in walked Elvis. He tried to say something, but the music was so loud we couldn't hear him. I walked over to the stereo and turned it off. Elvis said, "That's better; now you can hear me."

David said, "What's up, Elvis?"

Elvis said, "Not much. I was at the barn and heard y'all playing, so I thought I'd come in and sit in with you."

I said, "Sure. Grab a guitar and let's have some fun."

David joked, "You have to audition first before we'll let you play with us, man. We don't let just anyone off the street come in here and play."

Elvis broke out laughing, and so did I. He walked over, picked up a guitar, and said, "Do you know 'Little Sister'?" We both said yes, and Elvis instructed David to count it off. We jammed for about two hours that day. We played some of Elvis's songs, a few Zeppelin songs, and a couple of Grand Funk Railroad songs. David and I were amazed at Elvis's ability to listen to a song one time and play it perfectly.

When we finished, Elvis said, "That was fun, boys. Thanks for letting me sit in with you."

David said, "You passed the audition, but we do have another guy coming by later. We'll let you know if you made the cut."

Elvis and I laughed. David was joking, of course, because the reality was that Elvis towered above everyone else in terms of his musical energy.

It's ironic that the most legendary performer of the twentieth century once auditioned for the glee club in high school but didn't make it. They thought he wasn't a good enough singer. If they could have only seen how God was going to use this young man from Tupelo, Mississippi, to change the world with his music.

EIGHT

HE TOUCHED ME

Nearly every facet of Elvis's life has been explored and scrutinized in detail over the last few decades. The music, the movies, the fame, the controversies, the awards . . . everyone knows about those. But one of the few areas many people have not heard about is Elvis's generosity. I saw Elvis up close and personal for seventeen years, and I can tell you he is the most generous person I ever knew.

Vernon once told me something about Elvis I never knew. He said that when Elvis was a little boy, he would sometimes give his toys to the other children who didn't have anything. His parents even scolded him a couple of times because they had bought a toy for Elvis and he turned around and gave it away to someone less fortunate.

This didn't come as a surprise to me because that's exactly what Elvis was like as an adult.

Over the years, a lot of people have asked me, "Where did Elvis get his sense of generosity?" Elvis remembered what it was like being poor. He wanted to do everything possible to help other people avoid it.

I remember talking with him about his love of giving one time. He said, "Billy, it's not a sin to be rich, but it is a sin to love money. That's why I give so much of myself and what I have." Then he showed me Proverbs 11:25, which says, "A generous person will prosper; whoever refreshes others will be refreshed." Giving to others made Elvis feel happy and fulfilled. He loved the sensation of helping others.

He wrote in his Bible, "If one can't give what they have and share then they will always be empty." Elvis was more of a giver than a receiver. You might even say he was born to give. He never looked to any other star, athlete, or celebrity for how to live. He simply looked to Jesus. More than anything, Elvis wanted to be like Jesus in his actions, especially in the way he was generous.

Of all the memories I have of Elvis, this is one of my favorites.

One day Elvis said, "Let's go for a ride, Billy." Whenever Elvis said that, I would always grab his wallet and put it in my briefcase. The wallet had so much cash in it that you couldn't fold it, so my briefcase was the natural place to store it.

As we were driving, Elvis saw a man who looked like he was down on his luck. Elvis made a U-turn and drove up to the man. Before we got to him, Elvis said, "Get the money out of my wallet, Billy." I opened my briefcase, looked at the money and asked, "How much?"

"All of it."

Now, you have to picture this. Elvis's wallet was so full of money you couldn't bend it. I'd guess there was about $5,000 in it. As we pulled up to the man, Elvis told me to hand him the money. I did, and he stuck it between his legs so the man couldn't see it.

Elvis rolled the window down, and the man was surprised to see the King behind the wheel. Elvis asked, "How you doing, sir?"

"Well, my day is a lot better now that I've seen you, Mr. Presley."

"Please call me 'Elvis,' not 'Mr. Presley.'"

Then the man started telling Elvis how he had seen all of his movies and at one time had all of his records. Elvis thanked the man and asked again if he was doing okay. The man said, "I'm just a little down right now, but my luck is going to change soon."

Elvis said, "It already has." He took the money and reached out to give it to the man. At first, he thought Elvis wanted to shake hands. But when he saw the money, he said, "I can't take this, Elvis."

"Please take the money. It's my way of repaying you for watching all those silly movies." Elvis laughed.

The man started crying. "God bless you, Mr. Presley."

Elvis had tears in his eyes. "Sir, he already has blessed me." Then we drove off.

I began to cry also. I looked at Elvis and said, "That's the kindest thing I've ever seen, Elvis."

Then Elvis looked at me and said, "What good is having money if you can't help others?"

This kind of generosity was not unusual for Elvis. It was completely normal. I remember another time when I was with Elvis at a Cadillac dealership. He saw a couple on the parking lot, looking at cars. He asked the salesperson to have them come inside, then said to them, "Do you like the car you were looking at?"

The woman said, "No, we've got one already."

Then Elvis looked at the husband and said, "Well, sir, why don't you pick one out? You need one too." Then he bought the car for them.

∽

One time I took a date with me to Graceland, and it just happened to be the day that Elvis decided to buy cars for everybody. He had just given his cousin Patsy a Grand Prix to replace the Chevy Impala she had been driving. Elvis looked at my date and said, "What are you driving?"

She said, "I don't have a car."

Elvis motioned toward Patsy and said, "Take her car."

I told him, "This is only my first date with her."

He said, "Maybe it will help you."

After that, every time the girl saw Elvis, all she could do was say, "Thank you, Elvis, thank you, thank you." She absolutely loved that Impala.

He'd say, "Thank you, sweetie. It's no big deal. I'm glad you like it."

Elvis didn't only give to individuals. He also donated to thousands of charities during his lifetime. One year, the City of Memphis gave him a large wooden plaque to commemorate his contributions to more than fifty area charities. There are some publicity photos of him in the 1960s, writing checks to various charities.

However, he wasn't comfortable with the attention related to giving, which is why you never again saw photos of him writing checks. He didn't like being put in the spotlight for something he thought everyone should be doing.

One of the Bible verses that bothered Elvis was Matthew 19:24. Jesus said, "It is easier for a camel to go through the eye of a needle than for someone who is rich to enter the kingdom of God." He talked about this verse enough that I knew he was concerned about his heart being right. Elvis was a rich man, to be sure, but his heart was always in the right place. His generosity is world-famous, and he gave a large percentage of his money away.

Money didn't mean much to Elvis. It was just a means to make other people happy. Every day he looked for a way to give of himself and make people's lives better. In 2 Corinthians 9:7, the apostle Paul said, "God loves a cheerful giver."

If that's true, God must have really loved Elvis.

NINE

OH HAPPY DAY

What was it about Elvis that people loved so much? Was it the music? The movies? The energy? The charisma and personality? The glitz and glamour?

Perhaps all those play a part in Elvis's immense popularity during his lifetime and the decades since then. But they don't explain why people loved Elvis *so much*. Lots of entertainers have talent and charisma, but Elvis had something special.

As someone who spent lots of time with Elvis and got to know him on a level that few people ever did, I can tell you why his fans loved him so much. It's because he loved them first. Elvis was a generous man with his money, but he was also generous with his love. He injected passion and love into everything he did.

When he was in front of his fans and saw the looks on their faces as he was singing, it meant the world to him. He loved seeing their smiles and hearing their applause. Not because he wanted to be the center of attention, but because of how much love was going back and forth between him and his fans. Elvis lived for his fans, and it showed.

That's why he loved singing gospel music. It had more of a message than other songs just talking about having fun or being romantic. Elvis had more conviction about gospel music because he could share God's love with people in a way they would embrace. He loved them so much that he wanted them to know there is a God in heaven who loved them even more than he did.

Elvis was a living example of Colossians 3:23–24: "Whatever you do, work at it with all your heart, as working for the Lord, not for human masters, since you know that you will receive an inheritance from the Lord as a reward. It is the Lord Christ you are serving."

That's how Elvis approached everything in his life. There was no doubt about how much he loved God and how much he loved his fans. There are thousands of stories about Elvis interacting with his fans, but I'd love to share just a few.

When we first arrived at Graceland, my brothers and I would see people in the trees near the fence or standing at the front gates. We didn't know who they were or why they were there. We were so young we didn't know who Elvis was. We had no idea he was famous.

I remember the first time Elvis told me about the fans. I was eight years old and playing outside at Graceland. Elvis came out to play with me. As he walked toward me, he saw me waving my hand. When he got to me, he asked, "What are you waving at, Billy?"

I said, "The people in the trees. They have been waving at me all day. See?" Elvis looked over his shoulder and saw them. Now they were really waving and shouting Elvis's name.

He said, "Let's go say hello, Billy." Then he took me to the fence.

When we walked over there, everyone got excited. Elvis talked to them and signed autographs. He even introduced me as his little brother Billy, and I said, "Hi."

Everyone in the crowd said, "We love you, Elvis!"

He said, "I love you too."

After a while, he told the fans he wanted to teach me how to play football. Everyone thanked Elvis for coming over to talk to them. He said, "It was my pleasure, and I loved meeting you."

As we started to walk back to the yard, Elvis took my hand. I looked up at him and said, "Why do they love you so much, Elvis?"

He stopped walking and knelt down next to me. He said, "Do you see how much I love you?"

"Yes, sir."

"They see how much I love them too. I'm never too busy to stop and talk to them. They are the ones who made me what I am today."

"Well, the whole world must love you, because I see people every day in the trees and at the gates, even when it's cold outside. And everyone at school talks about you too."

He smiled. "So, if they love me, what should you do?"

"Love them too?"

Elvis hugged me, then said, "That's right, Billy."

I understood and said, "Okay." Elvis straightened up and we went to play football. I've never forgotten that lesson to this day. It's why I love Elvis's fans also.

∽

Sometimes Elvis showed his love for fans in more dramatic and public ways.

Later in his career, Elvis performed a song called "The Impossible Dream," written by Joe Darion and Mitch Leigh. By that point, my brother

David was working for Elvis. David knew that many of his fans resonated with the song. Who doesn't have an impossible dream?

Shortly before a concert, David spotted a little boy in a wheelchair who held up a sign that said, "THE IMPOSSIBLE DREAM." David is a huge guy on the outside, but on the inside he's like a gentle lamb.

David walked over to the little boy and asked, "What is your impossible dream?"

He said, "I want to meet Elvis."

David said, "I can make that happen. Wait right here." So, he went backstage and told Elvis about it. Elvis met with him for a few minutes to say hello. Then during the concert, he made sure the kid was right up next to the stage.

David always stood near the stage during the concert as a security measure. When Elvis and the band came to the song "The Impossible Dream," David got an idea. He grabbed another security person and they picked up the boy to place him onstage. Elvis loved it.

Another time we were doing a concert in New Mexico. I was working for Elvis, and we were told there would be a girl with a disability in the audience that night. As Elvis was about to go onstage, he said, "Is she there yet?"

His security detail backstage said, "No, not here yet."

Elvis said, "I'm not going on. I'm staying right here." The band had already been playing the first song intro, so they just kept going until the girl and her mother came and sat on the front row, where we had seats reserved.

After the concert, Elvis talked to them for a few minutes. We were leaving, and I was sitting in the limousine with him. He said, "I've sung before millions of people. But tonight, I sang for that one little girl." I don't think there was a dry eye in the car.

That's the kind of guy Elvis was. He couldn't handle the thought of a child hurting or being hungry, so he always did what he could. But it wasn't just children. He did it for everybody. Anyone who came in contact with Elvis could tell you how their life changed as a result . . . including Elvis impersonators!

∽

One day, after we had been with Elvis for quite a while, I was in the driveway at Elvis's LA residence. I looked toward the gates and saw someone dressed as Elvis. I thought Elvis might get a kick out of meeting one of his impersonators—also called tribute artists—so I went inside and told him about the guy.

Elvis said, "I've got to see this." We walked outside and up to the gates. Elvis began talking with the impersonator. They talked for a few minutes; then we went back inside. As we were walking back to the house, I asked Elvis, "What do you think of that?"

He said, "If someone wants to look like me and act like me onstage, more power to him. Imitation is the sincerest form of flattery."

I've met a few Elvis impersonators and worked with a couple. For the most part, I like them. The only ones I have a problem with are the ones who try to act like Elvis when they are offstage. Before and after the show, they try to imitate Elvis's voice and mannerisms. It's fine when you're onstage, but when you're offstage you should just be yourself.

I always enjoy meeting these impersonators and have fun at their shows, but it intimidates them because I grew up with the real deal. You might sound like him, act like him, and sing the same songs, but nobody can ever measure up to the one true Elvis.

∽

The one relationship that never let Elvis down was the one he had with his fans. He could always count on that. Elvis always knew that no matter what, his fans would never turn on him because he would never turn on them. That love affair went both ways because he would do anything in the world for a fan.

Back in the 1950s, there was a famous saying: "I'll give the fans the shirt off my back because they put a shirt on my back first." That's the kind of love he had for his fans. They were like family to him. They were he ones who had put him in his position and had made him into Elvis Presley the superstar.

Some people have said that Elvis was unlucky in love. That's not true, because there are millions upon millions of people who love that man. It's one love affair that never failed, and he was grateful for it.

When Elvis would pray, he would thank God for his fans. He would say, "Thank you for bringing them into my life." His thankfulness for his fans is why you see so many pictures of Elvis stopping to sign autographs for them. He didn't care if it would be an imposition.

He would be walking somewhere and a person would say, "Someone wants to meet you, Elvis." He would say "Okay" and take the time to stop and talk to anyone who wanted to chat with him. The conversation always started with how much they admired Elvis. They would always mention his music or some of his movies. Then he would thank them and ask what they did for a living.

After hearing what they did, he would say it was an admirable profession, no matter what it was. He would always take the conversation off him and put it onto the other person. For example, if he was talking to a construction worker, the conversation would go something like this:

"What do you do for a living?"

"I work construction."

Elvis would say, "You're the one who builds everything. You are important in this world. You are building the world we live in."

They could have been a president of a large corporation or a ditch digger. Elvis would always encourage them to be the best at what they did and share that the world needed them. He always said they were just as important as he was. It always amazed me to see how the person talking to Elvis would stand a little taller and feel better about themselves when they walked away.

To Elvis, the people of Memphis were more than fans. They had a special relationship with Elvis. He could go anywhere he wanted in Memphis and people wouldn't bother him. If they saw him, they just waved.

A friend told me one time, "Yeah, I saw Elvis out riding his motorcycle. I pulled up next to him in my car and said, 'Hey Elvis.' He looked at me and put his finger up to his mouth as if to say, 'Shh. Don't tell anybody.' Then we both laughed."

That's the way it worked in Memphis. People would wave to Elvis and he would wave back to them. The same was true when he went out to eat.

Where did Elvis get this impulse to love his fans and the people in his community? He got it from Jesus. When you read the Gospels in the Bible, you see Jesus stopping to talk to people. He didn't distinguish between the high and low people in society. He would talk with the lame, the sick, and the outcasts just as much as he would spend time with authorities or rich people.

Elvis tried to do the same thing. He talked to his fans whether he was out in public, on the road doing concerts, or literally in his own backyard.

Occasionally, someone will ask me, "Did Elvis know how much his fans loved him?" The answer to that is simple. Yes, he knew. How did he know?

He knew because his fans sent him more mail than anyone could count.

He knew because people bought his records. For decades Elvis was the #1 selling solo artist of all time.

He knew because the fans loved his movies. They weren't Hollywood blockbusters, but they made the studios a lot of money and entertained millions of people.

He knew because his concerts were always sold out.

He knew because he saw the love and emotion from fans when he was onstage.

He knew because of the notes. I have lots of firsthand knowledge of the notes that fans passed to him when he was performing. Trust me: they were full of love and devotion!

He knew because of the fans at the gates. When Elvis was at home, either in LA or at Graceland, fans were always waiting there, hoping to catch a glimpse of him or perhaps even talk to him. So yes, Elvis absolutely knew that his fans loved him. And he felt the same way about them.

But it wasn't just his fans. Elvis loved people in general. Whether it was entertaining fans, giving money to those in need, or taking time to have a simple conversation, he went the extra mile. For the most part, he was known as a man of peace, joy, and love. But on rare occasions when the situation called for it, he was not afraid to do whatever was necessary to defend and protect others.

PART 2

THE HOPE OF
HIS CALLING

TEN

WHERE NO ONE STANDS ALONE

One day in 1969, the *Memphis Press-Scimitar* reported the following incident:

> Elvis Presley used his fists to flatten a former employee during an argument, according to a county sheriff's office.
>
> A sheriff's office report Monday indicated the 31-year-old millionaire entertainer decked Jack Leonard, 33, with one blow. Leonard denied he had gone down but said Presley hit him twice.
>
> No arrests were made.
>
> The report said the incident occurred Sunday at the front gate of Presley's estate—Graceland, in suburban Whitehaven. Leonard was identified as a former yardman for Mr. Presley.

Elvis was not inclined to put up with trouble or grief from anyone. Even more so, he was a champion of racial equality. Here's the story behind this little-known incident.

A Black gentleman named Albert worked for the Graceland estate. He became ill and asked Vernon if he could take time off to recover. He planned to be gone for two or three weeks. Vernon said, "Yes, we'll be here when you get back."

So, Vernon hired a white worker named Leonard and told him, "As soon as the other person gets better, we're going to hire him back. This is just a temporary job."

Albert recovered and came back to work. When Vernon gave Leonard his last check, he said, "I'm sorry. This is your last one. You did a great job, and we appreciate you working with us. If you need any recommendations, I'll be happy to help." Vernon thought that was the end of it.

But Leonard decided it was not the end. One afternoon, he came to our house on Dolan Street and knocked on the door. When I answered, he said, "Can I speak with Vernon?"

I said, "Sure. Wait a minute." I walked to the den and told Vernon who was there. He got up and we both walked back to the door.

Leonard started in. "Why did you fire me?"

Vernon said, "I told you, it was a temporary position. We were waiting on Albert to come back. He's fine now, so we don't need any more help."

Leonard got mad and started cursing, saying, "How could you take a Black man over me?"

Vernon replied, "Color doesn't have anything to do with it. Albert's been with us a long time. He's a good man, and we plan on keeping him."

Leonard got even madder and continued to curse, using the N-word. Vernon said, "You'd better leave or I will call the police."

As Leonard stormed off, he said, "You haven't heard the end of this, mister."

Vernon and I walked back into the house. I asked him, "What do you think he'll do?"

He said, "Nothing. He's all talk."

It turned out he was more than talk. About thirty minutes later, we got a phone call from one of the guards at Graceland. "You better tell your dad to get over here. We've had trouble."

I was curious to see what had happened and rode with Vernon over there. We went up to the house and the guard said, "You need to see Elvis. He'll tell you what happened." We drove to the house and went into the den, where Elvis was sitting.

Elvis said, "I got a call from the guard. He said someone was at the gate, causing trouble. I went down to see what the trouble was. When I got there, this guy was cussing me and you, Daddy. He wanted to know why we fired him. I tried to calm him down, but he just wouldn't stop. Then he started using the N-word, so I said, 'That's enough. You don't need to be doing that.' I couldn't take it anymore, so I punched him in the mouth and told him if he ever came back around here, I would have him arrested."

Vernon and I looked at each other and smiled. Then Vernon looked serious and asked, "Do you think he'll come back or try to do something else?"

Elvis laughed. "No, Daddy. I think that's the last we'll see of him."

Sure enough, we never saw him again.

You never, ever used the N-word in front of Elvis. He would straighten you out so fast you wouldn't even know what happened. That might come as a surprise to some people who saw Elvis as a rich white man. But Elvis had grown up in a poor family of sharecroppers. You couldn't get any lower on the socioeconomic ladder than they were. Elvis treated everyone equally and didn't judge anyone by the color of their skin.

∞

Another word Elvis couldn't stand was *hate*. One time he told me, "Think about that word, Billy, and what it means. It's the opposite of love. To hate someone or something means you have no heart, no soul. You are empty of feelings."

He continued, "No one should go through life with hate. It will only lead you down a lonely, dark path. Only love can make everything okay. It will make your days better, not only for you, but for those around you. Love is the answer, Billy."

Elvis had another saying: "Use your X-ray vision when you talk to someone." He wanted us to look on the inside of a person, not the outside. He taught me to never look at anyone's skin or what kind of clothes they wear. I remember him saying, "That's not important, Billy."

"Then what is most important?"

He put his hand up to his chest, over his heart, and said, "This is what's important. That's what you look for. When I look at somebody, I see a person who is God's child. We are all God's children. It doesn't matter what skin color they have."

That's why Elvis was saddened and deeply hurt when Martin Luther King Jr. was assassinated in Memphis. He was ashamed of the city he loved so much. He said, "From now on, whenever you mention Memphis, it will always be associated with that tragic event."

Elvis admired Dr. King and thought he was a very wise man. He loved his "I Have a Dream" speech and felt his ideas about unity and equality were spot-on. Elvis saw him as a peaceful gentleman who was trying to improve life not only for Black people, but for everyone. He regretted that he had never gotten to meet Dr. King in person but tried to honor the ideals he had stood for in his song "In the Ghetto."

Vernon felt the same way Elvis did about equality. One time, when I was growing up, I had a conversation with Vernon about this issue. I asked, "What was it like when you lived in Mississippi, back in the days before Elvis was famous?"

He said, "Well, we never looked at anybody's skin color. We were no better than the sharecroppers, most of whom were Black. We lacked just as much as they did. When you grow up the same way as everybody else, you don't see skin color because you're all the same."

This attitude carried over to the day-to-day operations at Graceland, where the family had many Black employees who helped cook, take care of the grounds, and raise us boys. They were like our family. We didn't look at them any differently than we did Elvis's blood relatives.

Elvis didn't care where you were from or who you were. He treated everybody who worked for him the same.

Elvis's respect for Black people went far beyond his appreciation of Martin Luther King Jr. or the family's hiring practices at Graceland. He was so moved by Black gospel music that he incorporated the style into his signature hip-shaking moves.

He was emulating Black gospel singers and made no secret about it. Elvis said, "When the Holy Spirit reaches down and touches your belly, you can't stand still. You can't be quiet. Some people shout and scream and speak in tongues. But once the Holy Spirit touches you, it's the best thing in the whole world. You just can't sit still."

There were other artists at the time, such as Little Richard and Jerry Lee Lewis, who also used a lot of energy onstage and had a similar style at times. But Elvis was the one who popularized this style of performance.

Others came along after him, and he always said, "There's plenty of room in here. There are lots of people who can sing and do just as good as me or even better." Elvis always talked about Roy Orbison and how he was the best singer he'd ever heard. He said, "I would never follow that man onstage."

There was room for everyone in Elvis's world. He didn't focus on making life a competition or trying to fight for the spotlight. For Elvis, everything was about love. He tried to live by Jesus's words in John

13:34–35, which says, "A new command I give you: Love one another. As I have loved you, so you must love one another. By this everyone will know that you are my disciples, if you love one another."

Elvis would go to great lengths to demonstrate his love and loyalty to others. But as he progressed through the 1960s and found himself stuck in movie contracts that kept him from focusing on the music he loved, he found his love and loyalty being tested again and again.

ELEVEN

BY AND BY

Anyone who knew Elvis could tell you that he was a loyal man. You might even say he was loyal to a fault. Were all of Elvis's movies blockbusters? Of course not. Did Elvis himself know many of his movies, especially in the second half of the 1960s, were not that good? Yes, he did.

Colonel Tom Parker, Elvis's manager from the beginning, had kept his promise to make Elvis successful. However, "the Colonel," as he was known, had lost touch with the shift in popular tastes. People weren't as interested anymore in silly, predictable movies like the ones Elvis starred in most of the time. They had the same basic formula. Elvis usually played a little bit of a rebel. He gets into a fight and wins the girl. He sings a lot of songs along the way, and there is a happy ending.

Between 1956 and 1969, Elvis made a staggering thirty-three films—a lightning-fast pace by modern standards. But by the mid-1960s he had gotten tired of doing the same kinds of movies. He was at a point in his career where he wanted more dramatic roles.

As Elvis's manager, the Colonel was supposed to be looking out for

Elvis and creating new and exciting opportunities for him. But he no longer had his finger on the pulse of entertainment as he once had.

Elvis's movies still made money, even though no one considered them to be serious entertainment. As someone once said, the only sure thing in Hollywood was an Elvis movie. His movies made money so more movies could be made. It was an endlessly repeating loop, but it was in danger of becoming more and more irrelevant.

Elvis is best known for his music, but he was a gifted actor. I witnessed this firsthand, not just on movie sets with Elvis, but also at Graceland. He would read lines and memorize speeches and recite them. He also acted out the Bible for us sometimes, reading it and then portraying different characters in the passage.

His movie costars were also sometimes surprised at the range of his acting. After Elvis died, his *King Creole* costar, Walter Matthau, commented, "He was an instinctive actor . . . He was very elegant, sedate, and refined, and sophisticated."[1] Other actors and costars made similar comments. Many people considered Elvis quite a good actor, but he rarely had the opportunity for better roles due to the agreements locked in by the Colonel, who wanted him to stick with predictable "Mom and apple pie" roles.

One notable exception was 1969's *Charro!*, a western in the vibe of Sergio Leone's classic *The Good, the Bad and the Ugly*. Elvis was excited to play a different kind of role, and in fact grew a full beard for the movie—the only time he did this. *Charro!* was also the only movie where Elvis did not sing on-screen. It was an attempt at a little bit of serious acting. Elvis told me, "I thought I was really going to have a chance to do something serious here. But every time I had the chance to do something exciting, like draw my gun, instead of drawing it, I had to just give him a dirty look." He started to laugh.

Elvis didn't think much of his own movies, but there were other actors' movies he loved, like the *Dirty Harry* series. He wanted to play the lead in Barbra Streisand's *A Star Is Born*, but Colonel Parker killed that possibility. The Colonel thought it was too different from Elvis's usual type of movie role.

Despite his frustrations, Elvis tried to enjoy his time as a movie star. I remember him talking about a conversation he'd had with his costar Shelley Fabares on the set of *Clambake*.

He said, "One day I was sitting on set with Shelley and I just told her, 'You know, sweetie, we're not going to win any Academy Awards doing this stuff. So, let's just make it fun.'" And that's exactly what Elvis did. They would have squirt gun wars and water balloon fights on set because they needed something to break up the monotony. When you're on a movie set, it's mostly "hurry up and wait" while the crew sets up the next scene, adjusts lighting, or a hundred other things.

The producers and directors didn't care too much for Elvis's antics on set, but his attitude was, "What are they going to do? Fire me? I'm here to do your silly little movie, so let me have fun."

Elvis was always generous, trying to make it fun for the people in the movie. He could have done what so many movie stars did and sat alone in his trailer. But he told me that if any of his costars, or anyone else involved with the movie, ever wanted to talk to him, he would sometimes read a few verses of the Bible with them. Even on a movie set, God's Word was never far away from Elvis. It was in his heart at all times.

∾

The movies Elvis made started out as something fun. But they soon became so successful that by the time he received his draft notice in December 1957, he had contracts for several more Hollywood movies. However, by the time he had completed his Army service in March 1960, his future was uncertain. The only way the Colonel could think of getting Elvis's career back on track was to go right back to making movies.

The movie contracts wouldn't let him do live performances. Elvis did perform a couple of concerts for the Arizona Memorial in 1960 and 1961, as well as a couple of other live appearances, like going on *The Frank Sinatra Show*. But for most of the 1960s, Elvis focused exclusively on making movies.

The Colonel was concerned about Elvis having too much publicity. That seems crazy looking at it from today's point of view, but at that time there was a limited number of ways you could experience a celebrity. There were a few television channels, various radio stations, movies, and live concerts. That was pretty much it.

The Colonel didn't want to saturate the market with "too much Elvis." He thought three movies a year, plus a soundtrack to go with each one, was enough. That's not what Elvis wanted to do, but he always honored his contracts.

Some people believe that "the Colonel made Elvis." Not true. If the Colonel was responsible for Elvis's success, why didn't he help any other young stars rise to the same level of success?

Honestly, Elvis had outgrown the Colonel by the time the 1960s rolled around. If Elvis would have had better management, I believe his career would have taken a whole different trajectory. With a bigger variety of movies, he could have become one of the greatest movie stars of all time. But he saw the writing on the wall and knew that his opportunities in that field were limited as long as the Colonel was calling the shots.

That's why Elvis wanted to get off the silver screen and back onto the stage. His talent wasn't being put to its best use. As he said to me one time, "Billy, there's a big difference in people seeing me on a screen instead of me being on a stage, standing before them."

Elvis wrote a note to himself near the front of his Bible: "There is a season for everything, patience will reward you and reveal the answers to your questions." Perhaps he was thinking of Ecclesiastes 3:1 when he wrote that. It says, "There is a time for everything, and a season for every activity under the heavens."

Elvis had been patient long enough. His season of starring in movies would soon be coming to an end.

∞

On December 3, 1968, at 9:00 p.m. Eastern Standard Time, NBC viewers tuned in to witness something they hadn't seen in years: a live Elvis performance.

Colonel Parker had approached NBC over a year earlier to negotiate a Christmas special. He knew Elvis was wanting to get back to doing live music, and this was a way to do it without organizing a live concert. The Colonel had come to the network with specific ideas about the special, but Elvis balked at the thought of just doing a Christmas carol–themed show.

However, Steve Binder, the director, said, "Let's do it a different way." His idea was to make Elvis more relevant musically. After much discussion between Elvis, Steve, Colonel Parker, producer Bob Finkel, and NBC, they all finally agreed on an approach.

The special was officially titled *Singer Presents . . . Elvis* and showcased the King performing in three scenarios: in the round with a small acoustic band, in the round by himself, and in staged musical numbers. There was a lot of value in having him on television, but the special was also an experiment to see if he still had the Elvis magnetism he once had. Could he draw a crowd of television viewers?

The answer was a clear yes. The program was a massive hit and became a turning point in Elvis's career. The program became known as the *'68 Comeback Special*, but Elvis never liked that title. I remember one time when we were at the gates of Graceland and Elvis was signing autographs. A lady said, "I loved your Comeback Special."

Elvis replied, "I don't know what they mean by 'comeback.' Honey, I never went anywhere."

Indeed. Not only had Elvis not gone anywhere, but his presence was growing even stronger. The NBC special showed Elvis and millions of others that he still had it, that there was still a vast market for his live performances.

Where was the most obvious place to start doing live performances? Vegas, naturally.

Elvis had flopped in Vegas before, so there was a bit of concern. Back in 1956, Colonel Parker had set him up in Vegas, hoping to get him national attention. But in the 1950s, Vegas was still Sinatra's town. They still loved Sinatra, but the world had changed since then. Thirteen years later, in 1969, could Elvis make it work?

He did. He not only made it work—it was a stunning success. Elvis booked two shows a night for a month at the new Hilton. No performer had ever done that. He set the bar so high for other entertainers that most of them couldn't keep up with it.

That was typically the case with Elvis. No matter what he did, he was usually the first entertainer to do it. He was the first huge music star to transition to movies, the first to wear lots of jewelry (a trend that was later adopted by rap artists), and the first to do an acoustic set on a small stage in the round . . . decades before MTV began its *Unplugged* series.

Elvis could never rest on his laurels. He could never be content doing the same thing year after year. He had too much love for his fans, and for the talent God gave him, to stand still.

⚬∾⚬

The second half of the 1960s was a challenging time for Elvis. He was tired and creatively frustrated. Even though he wanted to be done with making movies long before he was, he honored his contracts while also making plans to get back to live concerts.

Elvis often prayed for the supernatural strength and guidance the prophet Isaiah talked about in Isaiah 40:28–31:

> Do you not know?
>> Have you not heard?
>
> The Lord is the everlasting God,
>> the Creator of the ends of the earth.
>
> He will not grow tired or weary,
>> and his understanding no one can fathom.
>
> He gives strength to the weary
>> and increases the power of the weak.
>
> Even youths grow tired and weary,
>> and young men stumble and fall;
>
> but those who hope in the Lord
>> will renew their strength.
>
> They will soar on wings like eagles;
>> they will run and not grow weary,
>> they will walk and not be faint.

Elvis was getting ready to soar again, personally and professionally. But unlike an eagle, he did not take to the skies alone. He preferred the company of his friends and family and was willing to do whatever was necessary to keep them safe.

TWELVE

STAND BY ME

Most of the people who worked for Elvis went to him when they had a problem of some kind. Whatever the situation was, he would fix it. He was always the one who took care of people, and he would be the first one willing to help. However, it bothered him that most of the people in his circle always seemed to want something from him. That's why I was careful to never ask him for money or any material items.

The only thing I ever asked Elvis to give me was his advice. I was just like every other young man who has questions, doubts, and insecurities. As my big brother, Elvis was my go-to source for wisdom. He had it all together. He was my hero.

Once I asked him how to deal with bullies.

He said, "First off, don't ever go looking for a fight. Nobody ever truly wins a fight. You might be standing up at the end, and the other guy is lying on the ground. But that doesn't mean you won. Anytime people get into a fight, that's a loss right there. But if it comes down to it, don't ever walk away from a fight."

I objected, "But the Bible says to turn the other cheek."

He said, "Well, you always try to. You can tell the other person, 'We don't need to do this. We don't have to fight.' Try to talk your way out of it first. But if he throws a punch and you get hit, don't just lie there and let somebody beat on you. Fight back."

I was in awe at his wisdom and confidence. He continued. "There's a time to be a lamb and a time to be a lion. You'll know when to be the lion."

Elvis had to deal with bullies too. One time he told us, "When I was growing up, I got bullied a lot because I wore my hair and clothes different than anybody else. There was always a kid who thought, 'If I beat this guy up, I'll impress my girlfriend.' I know about bullies."

Elvis wasn't kidding. He not only knew *about* bullies, but he also knew how to handle them personally. Elvis gave me a firsthand lesson one year when I was in high school.

One time I was dating a girl who had broken up with her boyfriend named James. He was a big defensive lineman who had gone off to college to play football. Every time I went out with the girl and he was back home, he would follow us around.

My brother Rick told Elvis about this. One night we were sitting at the table, finishing dinner. He said, "So Billy, I hear you've got a bully problem."

"What?"

"Yeah, Rick told me."

I looked at Rick as if to say, *Thanks a lot!*

Elvis continued. "I hear this guy's following you around. Sounds like he's a big football player."

"Yeah, he's just a big blowhard. Don't worry about it. I can take care of this."

"No, *I'm* going to take care of this. I can't stand a bully picking on one of my brothers. Where does this guy hang out?"

I was trying to think of something to say to keep Elvis from getting involved. I said, "We don't need to do this, Elvis. Thank you, but that's okay."

Elvis said, "No, we're going to take care of this tonight. Go get your car." Red, Sonny, and Lamar were there. Red and Sonny West were cousins who had been bodyguards for Elvis since the 1950s. Lamar Fike was a friend and lifelong employee who had also been with him from the beginning. All three performed a variety of duties for Elvis. "You guys go get the limo," Elvis told them. "Billy, you bring your car around front."

At the time, I was driving a 1957 Chevy, which I brought to the front. He got in the car with me and said, "Where does this guy hang out?"

There was a place in Whitehaven (south Memphis) where we used to cruise back and forth. A McDonald's and a Krystal restaurant sat about a block away from each other, and we would go cruising in that area. Elvis said, "Go to McDonald's first."

It was nighttime when we set out on this little adventure. As we pulled up, people could hear us before they would recognize us, since my car was a hot rod. Sure enough, a few of my friends were standing there. When they saw the car, I slowed down and they started walking toward it. They saw who was sitting with me and said, "Hey, Elvis! How you doing, bud?"

Elvis replied, "Hey, nice to meet you guys." We exchanged high fives as Elvis sat there with me.

One of the guys said, "What are y'all doing?"

Elvis said, "We're looking for James."

My friend replied, "Well, he was here just a few minutes ago. He might be down at Krystal." I looked at the guy as if to say, *Thanks a lot, buddy.*

Elvis said, "Well, it's nice to meet you guys. We're gonna head down there."

So, we drove down to the popular burger place, where the same thing happened. But this time, the kids hanging out there said, "Well, he left. We don't know where he went." We started heading back toward Graceland.

There was an Ace Hardware parking lot between McDonald's and Krystal. We thought it was cool to sit on the lot with our parking lights on to let people know we were hanging out. As we drove by, Elvis said, "You know any of those guys over there?"

"Yeah."

"Pull in there."

I thought, *Oh great.* I pulled in, and a few friends came running up to the car. They had never seen Elvis riding around with me and were surprised to see him sitting there. They said, "Hey Elvis, how you doing? Great to meet you."

Elvis replied, "Hey guys. How's it going? Nice to meet you guys."

One of my buddies said, "What are y'all doing?"

Elvis said, "We're looking for James. Any of y'all know where he lives?"

One guy said, "Yeah, I know." Then he gave me the address.

Elvis turned to me. "You know where that is?"

"Yeah."

"We're going over."

One of my buddies said, "You need any help?" This was laughable because Elvis clearly didn't need any help.

He said, "No, buddy, I think we can handle this ourselves."

As we pulled away, all I heard was, "James is in for it now!" I was trying to imagine what Elvis was going to do when he saw this guy. I had no idea what to expect.

We drove to the house and pulled in the driveway with the limo behind us. Elvis said, "Okay, Billy, you're going with me. Red, Sonny, Lamar, wait right here."

We walked to the front of the house and rang the doorbell. James's mother opened the door and had a look of total surprise when she saw Elvis standing there.

"Elvis!"

"Yes, ma'am."

"Uh . . . can I help you?" She couldn't seem to find her words, probably wondering, *Why is Elvis Presley standing in my doorway?*

"Is your son home, ma'am?"

"Yes, sir."

"Just call me Elvis."

"Okay, Elvis. I'll get him. Hang on a second."

She closed the door, and a moment later, both parents stood there as James walked up behind them.

Elvis turned to James's father. "Nice to meet you. I've got a few words for James." They stepped aside as he came to the front. Elvis continued, "I understand you've been following my little brother here, Billy, around."

When he said that, the parents looked at James. It was a funny sight to see his parents giving a questioning look to their son, who was a six-foot-four, 260-pound defensive lineman.

His father said, "Have you been doing this?" He didn't even give his son a chance to say anything.

James admitted, "Yes, sir."

His father was about to say something, but Elvis broke in.

"No, sir, let me finish. If that ever happens again, I want you to understand I'm coming over here, and it won't be talking next time. You understand that?"

His parents were nervous. "Mr. Presley . . ."

"No, call me Elvis."

His father spoke. "You don't have to ever worry about that. I promise he will never follow your brother again."

Elvis turned to James. "Now, what have you got to say, James?"

"Okay. I promise I won't follow him around anymore."

"I'm going to hold you to that."

His parents were being nice and apologetic. You could tell they felt bad about what had happened. Elvis said, "Everything's taken care of. There's no problem. But if it happens again, if I have to come back here, it ain't gonna be nice."

They said, "Don't worry. You'll never have to come back here, we promise."

Elvis shook their hands and said, "It's nice to meet you. I'm sorry it was under these circumstances. I hope you all have a good night."

As they closed the door and we walked away, we heard yelling inside the house. I looked at Elvis and thought, *Wow. He just did that for me.* We climbed into the car and he started laughing. He said, "Man, did you hear his parents?"

"Oh yeah. They gave him an earful! That's for sure."

"Hopefully, this will settle your problem."

"Yeah, I think it did, Elvis. Thank you for doing this. You didn't really have to do it. I could have handled it."

Elvis laughed. "Billy, that guy could break you in half. Don't even kid yourself. You saw how big he was."

"I bet his dad is wearing him out right now," he went on. "His mom wasn't a big lady, but she's probably the one that's beating him the worst." We laughed all the way back to Graceland.

And just like that, I never saw James again.

I share this story to illustrate that the Elvis we knew in private was much the same person as the one the world knew—tough, charismatic, and didn't take any guff from anyone, including people who threatened to harm people he loved.

It reminds me of Proverbs 17:17, which says, "A friend loves at all times, and a brother is born for a time of adversity." When Solomon wrote those words nearly three thousand years ago, he didn't have Elvis in mind. But I can't think of any words that better describe how I feel about my big brother.

As Elvis progressed in his career, he would go through lots of ups and downs, times of triumph and times of adversity. That's why he needed a group of guys, an inner circle, who had *his* back. For years, I had dreamed of being part of this group. I had waited long enough.

THIRTEEN

I'VE GOT CONFIDENCE

Elvis was a musical force of nature. Anytime you see recordings or films of him performing, his charisma practically jumps through the screen. To the untrained eye, it probably seems like Elvis single-handedly carried the energy of the whole affair squarely on his shoulders.

Elvis almost always had a band and backup singers, but there was more to his success than that. He employed an entourage of people who helped him in every capacity. They enabled him to perform, travel, and focus on making music.

Most of his crew had been with him since the 1960s, a couple of them since the 1950s. I grew up with these guys. They were like an extended family to me. So, I was thrilled to become a part of the group when I joined Elvis's payroll in 1969.

This happened almost by accident. Whitehaven was a very well-to-do neighborhood back then, and all my friends were getting allowances. It's all they talked about at school.

One day, I thought I'd test the waters and see if I could get an allowance also. I went to the office at Graceland and asked Vernon about it, but it immediately came to a crashing halt. Vernon said, "You can't have an allowance, but I'll get you a mower so you can mow the yards."

I walked out of the office with a dejected look on my face. Elvis just happened to be walking by and noticed my expression. He said, "What's wrong?"

I told him I'd asked Vernon for an allowance.

He laughed and said, "How did it go?" Elvis already knew what Vernon would say before I even replied. Then he said, "Let's go back in there and talk to him."

I followed Elvis into the office. He said, "Daddy, let's put Billy on the payroll."

Vernon said, "Okay. What's he going to do?"

Elvis stood there for a moment. "He can wash my cars twice a week."

"How much do you want to pay him?"

"Two hundred dollars a week."

"What?" Vernon thought that was outrageous.

Elvis laughed. "No, Daddy, I'm just kidding. Give him a hundred dollars a week." In one fell swoop, Elvis negotiated a deal that solved my allowance problem, gave me some responsibility, and addressed Vernon's concerns. That was the beginning of my employment for Elvis. I think I only washed the cars once a week.

Three years later, I joined the touring crew. Rick and David had joined before I did, even though I was older. I loved being able to go out to Vegas on summer vacation and stay a couple of weeks with the crew, but I had no aspirations of working for Elvis. When I was growing up, I wanted to be a mechanic and race cars. Working for Elvis would have taken me away from that.

Plus, when I was a kid, we moved all the time, since my birth father was in the military. I had to make new friends constantly. So, when we came to Memphis in 1960 and put down roots there, I didn't want to leave.

Rick and David kept saying, "Billy, come on, man. You gotta join us. It will be the four of us together." Finally, I relented.

When I joined, the first thing Elvis did was call me up to his room. I didn't know what was going on. I was half expecting a surprise wrestling match. It wouldn't have been the first time that happened.

I went upstairs and saw Rick and David in the room with Elvis. Rick was grinning from ear to ear and had his hand behind his back. Elvis said, "Okay, Billy, it's about time this took place." Then he motioned to Rick, who handed him a little black jewelry box.

I thought to myself, *Could this be what I think it is?*

He said, "Billy, it's time for you to become part of the tribe. I present you with this TCB. Wear it proudly." He opened the box and took out a necklace with the letters *TCB* hanging at the bottom. This stood for "Taking Care of Business," which was a motto Elvis often used. It meant that we took care of business lightning fast.

Elvis placed the necklace around my neck. I was so happy that a few tears came to my eyes. I had seen the other guys working for Elvis wear their TCBs for a few years, and I wanted one too. But I couldn't ask for one. I never asked Elvis for anything except advice.

Elvis, Rick, and David saw how happy I was and congratulated me. Rick and David patted me on the back and welcomed me aboard. We ended the celebration with a group hug. Then Elvis said, "There's no turning back now, Billy." Rick and David agreed. I was now part of Elvis's inner circle.

And thus began my initiation into the legendary Taking Care of Business crew.

∞

As the TCB crew, we were Elvis's personal aides and security detail. We were always on call, twenty-four hours a day, seven days a week. If Elvis wanted something, we took care of it. If he wanted to talk to someone on the phone, we called them. If he wanted something to eat, we got it for him.

When we were on tour and he wanted new shirts, he'd send us to get them. We'd always ask what color or design, and he would say, "I trust your judgment. Pick whatever you think." He was always pleased with what we got for him.

We also knew Elvis's schedule each day. He would usually tell us who was coming to see him that day and ask us to tell him when they arrived. Sometimes he would tell us he didn't want to see a particular person.

Elvis would also test us by asking for something like a cheeseburger at three or four in the morning. When we came back, he'd say, "I'm not hungry now. I just wanted to make sure you were on duty." Then he would laugh and ask us to sit and talk with him.

Whenever Elvis was in public, we always made sure he had a glass of water. If he wanted a cigar, we had it handy. If he wanted some chewing gum, it was there. He never had to ask because we always had those things ready for him. We took a lot of pride in anticipating Elvis's needs and making him look good in front of other people. He would always give us a wink after we had done something without him having to ask.

One time the four of us—Elvis, me, Rick, and David—were standing in his dressing room, helping him get ready for a show, and that's when he gave us the nickname "the Wrecking Crew." From that point on, anytime Elvis wanted the three of us, there was no mistaking who he was talking about. We were a separate entity from the TCB group.

The Wrecking Crew was also responsible for "tearing down" Elvis. Every time he came offstage, we had to get him out of his clothes, get him in the shower, get him dressed, and bring him back out if he needed to meet others or sign autographs. Elvis could have done all these things himself, but when you're a superstar on the level of Elvis

Presley, you always have an entourage who helps you with even the smallest details.

This was especially important because time was of the essence. When you have a crew helping you come offstage and doing all the things necessary to get you ready for whatever comes next, it goes much faster. In a way, you're a king.

One of my most important jobs was making sure Elvis's Bible was with him at all times. When we were on tour, the Bible went with him everywhere. Elvis was a Bible-carrying believer and proud of it.

Being a part of TCB, as well as the Wrecking Crew, made an incredible difference in my confidence. I learned how to be more responsible and take care of other people's needs, not to mention all the real-world experience you get being on tour with a major artist.

∞

Being a part of the Wrecking Crew on the road with Elvis was not all work. We had loads of fun together. Elvis could be like a little kid at times, always thinking of ways to entertain himself and make others feel at ease.

One day in 1972, when we were in Vegas, it was my turn to wake up Elvis. Rick, David, and I were sitting in Elvis's hotel suite in the den. Both of them said, "Get to work, rookie."

I laughed and said, "Okay."

I walked into Elvis's bedroom, then approached his bed. I said, "Time to get up, Elvis." He didn't respond. I said it again. Still no response.

I thought, *Maybe I should shake him. That might work.* I shook him and said again, "Time to get up, Elvis." Still no response. Then I thought, *Maybe Rick and David could tell me what to do.* So, I went back into the den and told them my problem. They both smiled at me. Then they started giving me a hard time.

Rick said, "Just a rookie!"

David said, "We get you a great job, and what do you do? You ask us for help."

I laughed at them. I knew they were loving this moment. I said, "C'mon. Please help me. I don't know what to do."

They both stood up and said, "We'll help you this time, but don't ever ask us again. You got that, rookie?"

I laughed at them. I had to go with the moment, so I sheepishly replied, "Okay." That busted them up, they laughed at me again, and we all three walked into Elvis's bedroom.

When we got to the bed, Rick said, "Time to get up, Elvis." No response.

I said, "I've already tried that, Rick."

David said, "Y'all get outta the way. I'll show you how it's done." He walked to the bed, shook Elvis, and said, "Hey, it's wake-up time, Elvis."

That didn't work either. I said, "I tried that also."

The three of us stood there thinking. Rick looked over at the end table and saw the glass vase where we would put Elvis's bottled water. The ice had melted overnight, and there were three bottles still in it. Rick pointed to it. We all three looked at each other, then a smile came to our faces.

I said, "Really?"

David said, "Heck yes!"

I took a deep breath, then said, "Okay, let's do it." Rick took out the bottles of water and picked up the vase. Rick said, "No turning back now," then threw the water on Elvis.

He came off that bed so fast we didn't have a chance. A wrestling match broke out. It looked like something out of WrestleMania. There were no sworn allegiances. Elvis would be on top of me, and Rick and David would be pulling on him. Then Elvis would get on David, and Rick and I would get on Elvis. Bodies were flying everywhere.

When we finished, all four of us were lying on the floor, dead tired and laughing. Elvis was laughing so hard he started crying. A couple of other guys from the crew came running into the bedroom. I guess they had heard us and didn't know what was going on, which made us laugh even more.

Aside from the epic wrestling match, one other great thing happened that day. From that moment on, every time we tried to wake up Elvis, he woke up.

There was never a dull moment when you worked for Elvis. He was full of surprises and never pulled his punches. But he knew his place in the universe and was always asking for God's help.

When Elvis was doing a concert, he always said a prayer before walking out onstage. Many people would be surprised to learn that Elvis was nervous before performing. Once, when we were in Vegas, I asked him, "Why are you so nervous, Elvis?"

He said, "Each show is like a first date, Billy. I want the date to be perfect."

I reassured him he would do great, then he smiled as he walked onstage.

Another night soon after that, we were standing at the side of the stage. Elvis was doing his routine. After he prayed, he hit me. I said, "Elvis, what did you do that for?"

He said, "Hit me on the shoulder."

I asked, "Why?"

Elvis gave me a stern look and said, "Hit me, Billy."

I gave him a funny look and punched his shoulder. It wasn't a very hard hit. So, he looked at me and said, "Is that all you have?"

I thought to myself, *Okay. You asked for it*. I hauled off and hit him again, much harder this time.

He smiled, then said, "Thanks, Billy." He put his arm around my shoulder and we stood together as his entrance song was coming to an end.

When he took his first step toward the stage, he turned suddenly, then hit me on the shoulder. He tagged me pretty good too. I grabbed my shoulder, then turned to punch him back. Then he turned around and walked onstage.

As he stepped into the spotlight, he looked back at me, smiling as he made his entrance. I was happy that I'd helped him forget about his nerves before he took the stage that night. Even if it did hurt!

If I had to choose one Bible verse that describes how Elvis shaped my confidence and attitude, it would be Proverbs 13:20, which says, "Walk with the wise and become wise, for a companion of fools suffers harm."

In the seventeen years I spent with Elvis, especially as part of his touring entourage and the Wrecking Crew, one of the ways he helped me become wiser was to continually build my confidence. One time he said, "Everyone needs to be self-confident. If you don't believe in yourself, no one else will either."

I said, "You're Elvis-freaking-Presley. It's easy for you to say that!"

He laughed, then got serious. He said, "Billy, do you think I got here by not believing in myself? No one believed in me. I mean, no one. Not even Daddy. But I stayed true to myself and followed my heart. I knew I could make it, if only given a chance."

"But what about you being discovered at Sun Records? They believed in you."

"No, they didn't. They asked me to come in and record a song. They didn't like the way I was singing it, so they took a break. I thought I was done. So, while we waited for them to come back, I asked the guys to play a song. But I said, 'Let's play it like I wanted to.' I told them how to play it. The next thing I knew, everyone in the booth said, 'Play that song again, but play it the way you were doing it when we came in.' That's how it all started, Billy."

"Wow. I never knew that."

"Most people don't know that. But I was given a chance to do what I heard in my head, not what everyone else wanted me to do."

"What does that have to do with self-confidence?"

Elvis shook his head in disbelief, then said, "I knew, if given the chance to do the music in my head and heart, people would like it. At least that's what I hoped."

"You were right. Everyone loves it."

Elvis smiled. "If I hadn't believed, no one would be listening today." He paused and then said, "Everyone has a gift, something they are good at. They just need someone to encourage them to never give up and to believe in themselves."

When I first came into Elvis's life, I suffered from what he called a "terminal case of shyness." The whole time I knew Elvis, he kept helping me develop self-confidence. He would say, "There's nothing you can't do, Billy. When you rely on God's strength, you can do anything in this world. It's not just me on your side. It's God on your side too. With God, all things are possible."

When my brothers and I were kids, Elvis watched out for us. As we got older, we had the privilege of helping watch out for him as part of the TCB and the Wrecking Crew. I can't imagine where my life would be today if not for Elvis's influence and wisdom. Through every kind of experience you can imagine, we sharpened each other. As a result, we were all better, stronger, and faster.

But nothing made me go faster, and no bond was stronger, than when Elvis and I hopped into one of his fast cars.

FOURTEEN

SWING DOWN, SWEET CHARIOT

During my seventeen years with Elvis, we bonded over many different experiences. I grew up in the same home as him. I went on tour with him and was part of his crew. I saw him fall in love, get married, and have a child. I was with him through countless highs and lows.

But there was one bond we shared that was stronger than any other: driving fast cars.

Ernest Hemingway said, "There are only three sports: bullfighting, motor racing, and mountaineering; all the rest are merely games." Elvis and I never stood in a ring with bulls or climbed a mountain together, but we loved racing. And it was far more than a game to us.

The love of speed is something you're born with. It's in your blood. Elvis and I had countless conversations about racing and why we loved it. It all came down to one factor—the feeling you get when you are pushing the car's limits.

When Elvis or I got into a car, it was like putting on a jacket or shirt.

The car becomes an extension of you. You feel the engine and it becomes your heartbeat. Your senses extend to each part of the car. You feel what the tires are doing in the corners. The steering wheel is like your eyes. It will take you in the direction you want to go.

Some drivers like to use the tachometer, which measures engine speed. Some racing drivers also use a shifting light, which indicates that you've reached maximum revolutions per minute. That doesn't mean they aren't good drivers, but Elvis and I never used either. Why? Because we could feel or hear the exact point in the engine cycle when we needed to shift to the next gear. It's called "seat of your pants" driving. That was our style.

I've heard some say that racing is flirting with death, and that's the thrill of it. Others have said the thrill is being in control of something that's out of control. None of that made any sense to Elvis or me.

For us, it was all about the adrenaline rush. No drug could give us the same feeling as being one with the car. All we wanted was the sensation of the engine screaming as you bang through the gears, hitting the apex just right and flying through a corner.

The only people who can understand this are the ones who have experienced the thrill of racing. It's like trying to explain an Elvis concert. If you never saw one, you will never know the thrill of experiencing it for yourself.

As our mentor, Elvis knew the best way to teach us about life was to get us into active situations where we could experience life firsthand. In my case, Elvis used cars and racing as a way for us to build a close relationship.

Young men have always wanted to feel the sensation of the wind on their faces as they speed through God's creation. For thousands of years, people had to rely on manually propelled boats or horses and chariots to give them speed.

Elvis and I sure loved driving our chariots! Or in Elvis's case, it could be his Ferrari, Stutz, or '53 panel truck, depending on his mood.

Racing is all about the sensation of speed. Once you get hooked on it, the only way to satisfy that craving is to climb into a fast car and get moving. But other than the speed, what was it about cars that Elvis loved so much? Why did he spend so much time, energy, and money on this hobby?

Elvis loved the independence a car gave you. When you turn sixteen and finally get your driver's license, your world gets much bigger. You can go places without having to ask anyone. It's the first time you experience any true freedom in your life.

For the first sixteen years, you're around your parents the whole time. But when you turn sixteen, you have a means to go out and do things apart from them. You have freedom, but that's where trust comes in. If your parents have raised you correctly, they don't have to worry. So, in a strange sort of way, that freedom helps ensure your parents will make sure they raise you right.

That feeling of freedom, of independence, is one of the reasons Elvis gave away so many cars. He loved to see the expression on people's faces when he gave them something. He knew the excitement the other person was feeling when he gave them a car, jewelry, or money, because he had experienced it himself. And he wanted to do that for others.

Racing was a way for Elvis to bond with me. He had different ways to bond with different people, but Elvis was especially passionate about cars. He saw that I loved cars, and it was simply an entry point into my world and the things I cared about. It was a connecting point with me, a way for him to mold and shape me. One of the nicknames Elvis gave me was "Gearhead" because of my love for cars and motorcycles.

The time I spent with Elvis constantly sharpened and polished me. He never held back. He didn't hold back his love, his money, his passion, or his love for God.

And he never held back when it came to speed.

The famous race car driver Mario Andretti once said, "If everything seems under control, you're not going fast enough." Elvis tested this philosophy more than once.

When Elvis bought a Ferrari Dino, I asked if I could take it for a ride around town. He said, "I know what you want to do, Billy, but it's not going to happen this time."

I smiled at him. He was right. He knew I was going to run the heck out of that car. I said, "I just thought I'd take it to the car wash. It's starting to get a little dirty."

Elvis laughed at me and said, "Nice try." Then he said, "Let's go for a ride, Billy. Let me show you how fast it is." Whenever Elvis was considering buying a car, that's the first thing he would ask. "How fast is it?"

We hopped into the Dino and drove down Elvis Presley Boulevard to the entrance of I-55 South going toward Mississippi. Back in the day, it was like most interstate highways—two lanes with a median that had gravel on both sides of the pavement. As we drove onto the entrance ramp, Elvis said, "Hang on."

I jokingly said, "Okay," and Elvis looked over at me with a sneer. That made me laugh. Elvis slammed the Dino into second gear, and we took off. We were both pinned to our seats as the car rapidly picked up speed. Then he shifted into third, and we slammed into the seats again. Then he went to fourth.

The g-forces were starting to ease up, and we were going pretty fast now. I watched Elvis as he was driving and looking out the side window to get the sense of speed. He smiled and then shifted into fifth gear. I was loving it, and so was Elvis.

He looked over at me and then pointed to the speedometer. I looked and was surprised to see we were going 160 miles per hour. I jokingly said, "I thought this thing was supposed to be fast, Elvis." He just laughed.

As I said that, I looked ahead and saw a semitruck in the right-hand lane, which we were in. Elvis saw it also, and we moved to the left lane. Just as we moved, we saw the truck move over also.

There were two trucks in front of us, and we were rapidly approaching them. We were still going 160. When you're going that fast, you can't just hit the brakes. You have to ease up on them. Elvis did that, but we were still going 145 miles per hour when we got to the trucks.

Elvis eased the car onto the left-side median. Gravel started hitting the undercarriage of the car. I thought to myself, *This is it. Elvis and I are about to die. But at least we'll die doing something we love.*

I could see the newspaper headline the next day: "Elvis and Brother Die in Horrible Car Crash." But then, to my relief, he steered the car around the semis and got it back up on the interstate.

The Dino stayed straight as we passed the semis. Elvis brought it back onto the highway, and we both looked at each other and took a deep breath. The Dino was slowing down. When we got to the legal speed limit, Elvis said, "Well, I think that'll be enough for today, Billy. What do you think?"

"Yeah, Elvis. I think so too." We both laughed.

The drive back to Graceland was slow and quiet. Neither one of us said anything for a long time. But when we pulled into Graceland and got out of the car, Elvis looked at me and paused for a moment. Then he said, "Was that fast enough for you, Billy?"

"Not really, Elvis."

We both laughed and walked into the house.

∽

Racing wasn't just about having a good time or narrowly escaping death. Elvis used all kinds of crazy circumstances to build my confidence and teach me a thing or two.

Before Elvis bought the *Lisa Marie*, his private jet, he would fly commercial flights to LA. One time he needed to get to the airport in about twenty minutes. As we were leaving, Vernon said, "Who's going to drive the second car?" This was for the crew who didn't ride with Elvis.

Elvis looked at me and gave me a wink. "Let Billy do it." He asked me to take the Cadillac limo, and Ricky and Charlie joined me.

For some reason, Charlie was late getting to the car. When Charlie jumped into the limo, he and Ricky told me, "You have to catch them, Billy, or we'll miss the flight."

That's all I needed to hear, so I floored it.

We roared out of the gates at Graceland like a bullet from a gun. We turned right onto Elvis Presley Boulevard but couldn't see Elvis's car. I floored the gas pedal, and Ricky and Charlie encouraged me to go faster. I was happy to oblige.

When we came to the corner at Elvis Presley Boulevard and Winchester Road, the light was red, so I cut through a gas station that used to be there. As I turned onto Winchester, the limo was almost on two wheels. I continued down Winchester until we got to the airport.

As we pulled onto the tarmac, we could see Elvis's car ahead of us. Everyone in the car was looking back at the limo. As they came to a stop, I pulled up beside them and parked. Everyone was laughing when they got out of the car. Elvis walked over to me and said, "Doggone it, Gearhead! Everyone said you wouldn't make it here on time, but I told them you would. I knew you could do it, Billy." He smiled and gave me a hug. Then he laughed and said, "I guess those racing lessons I gave you paid off."

I laughed and said, "Yeah, they sure did, Elvis. They sure did." I'll never forget the look on his face that day and the pride he showed in what I had done.

We liked to go fast, and most of the time we were able to avoid getting caught by the police. But occasionally we weren't so lucky.

One time I was at Graceland, working on one of my cars, a Chevy

Chevelle. I had just finished changing out the plugs when Elvis walked over. He said, "How fast does it go?"

"Faster than you want it to go."

"Well, let's just see about that."

I smiled and said, "All right" and closed the hood. Elvis jumped in the driver's seat, I got into the passenger seat, and we backed out. I don't know if the skid marks he left are still there at Graceland, but I know they were there for years. Once we backed up and started heading toward the gate, Elvis floored it and those back tires lit up.

"This thing's pretty good!"

"Thanks!"

We drove down the hill, went out the gate, and then took a right. Elvis floored it. We were hauling, banging through the gears, and life was good, with the windows down and wind blowing in our hair. I could see a huge grin on Elvis's face.

He was just about to shift into fourth gear when he started slowing down. I said, "This has got a lot more. Why did you let off?"

Elvis pointed at the rearview mirror. I looked back, and sure enough, there was a policeman on a motorcycle. We pulled over and Elvis said, "I'll handle this."

The policeman walked to the car, probably ready to stick it to the driver. But then he saw who was driving and said, "Elvis?"

"Yes, sir."

"What are you doing driving this thing?"

Elvis motioned to me and said, "Well, this is my little brother's car. This is my little brother Billy right here."

I leaned forward and waved to the policeman. He asked Elvis, "What are you doing?"

Elvis said, "I'm showing him how not to drive this thing on the highway."

Then Elvis and the policeman started laughing. I nervously chuckled, but I didn't want to take it too far since I didn't know what might happen. I didn't think we were going to jail or anything, but I figured we might get a warning. If that was the case, I knew Elvis wouldn't ask for special treatment because he didn't take advantage of situations like that.

The policeman thought for a moment. Then he said to Elvis, "Well, do you think he learned his lesson?"

I leaned forward and said, "Yes, sir, I did."

We both started laughing, and he began, "Okay, Mr. Presley—"

Elvis interrupted him. "Please call me Elvis."

"Okay, Elvis. Just don't do anything foolish like this on my shift. I would hate to call in that Elvis Presley was in a car wreck or something like that."

"Don't worry about it, sir. I'll never do it again."

The policeman walked away and we headed back toward Graceland.

That was pure Elvis—always protecting others, always respectful of law enforcement, and always enjoying life.

And most of all, teaching me how *not* to drive a fast car on the highway.

FIFTEEN

LEAD ME, GUIDE ME

With Elvis as my teacher and mentor, class was always in session. No topic was off-limits, including one I was especially interested in as a teenager: girls.

I remember a talk we had with Elvis around 1971, when I was eighteen. It was one of those "big brother" types of talks. Elvis, Rick, David, and I were watching TV. As we were watching, a question came to mind. I asked Elvis, "Did you ever date any of your costars?"

He gave a sly smile. "What do you think?"

"Yeah, I think you did. I mean, who wouldn't? They were all beautiful."

"You are correct, young one." We all laughed and started asking about his leading ladies. Rick would ask a few questions, David would ask a few, then it would come back to me. I could see Elvis was having a good time, being the older brother. Of all the roles he played, this was one of his favorites.

After talking about his leading ladies, the conversation turned to dating. Elvis started giving us advice on how to treat a girl. The first thing he said was, "Women are a gift from God, and that's the way they should be treated." Then he said, "Be protective of women. They should feel comfortable and not be afraid of anything happening to them while they are with you. Make them laugh. If you can do that, they will love you forever."

I had never heard that advice before. "Really? Making a woman laugh is that important?"

"You can bet on that, Billy."

I shook my head. "Okay, I'll remember that."

Our conversation lasted for about an hour as we talked about all of his leading ladies. Elvis was really into teaching us about dating and women. Vernon came in and said he needed to talk to Elvis.

Elvis stood up. "Okay, boys. That's it for today's lesson. We'll talk more about this sometime." Then he got up and walked away with Vernon.

My brothers and I sat there for a little while and talked about what Elvis had said to us. We were amazed he had talked about all of his costars and was so open about it. He told us everything. Then Rick said, "He did that because he knows we won't tell anyone what he said." David and I nodded in agreement.

Whenever I see comments on fan pages about Elvis's leading ladies, and what they *think* Elvis felt about these women, I always laugh and think to myself, *If you only knew . . .*

Elvis had years of experience dealing with the opposite sex, including many of the world's most famous women. Me and my brothers, on the other hand, were just beginning to learn. We made our fair share of mistakes.

One night, a few years later, Rick and I were cruising around Whitehaven in Elvis's Lincoln Mark IV. We weren't doing much, just riding around. I noticed a blue light on the floor of the car and said, "I wonder what it would be like pulling someone over with this?"

Rick said, "I don't know. It depends on who you pull over." He thought for a moment and said, "It might be a good way to meet some girls."

I laughed. "You may be right. Let's try it."

For the next hour or so, that's what we did. We pulled over cars with girls, but most of them just drove off when we walked up to their car. They took one look at Rick and me, with our long hair, and knew it was some kind of joke. A couple of them even got angry. Most of them just laughed and thanked us for not giving them a ticket.

When we got back to Graceland, Elvis was waiting on us. We could tell he wasn't in a good mood. He told us to follow him upstairs, which we did. He walked over to his desk, took a seat, and told Rick and me to have a seat.

When we sat down, he said, "I got a call from the police a little while ago. They said two long-haired guys were pulling over women."

Rick and I looked at each other, then back at Elvis. "That was us, Elvis."

"I know it was y'all, but did you ever stop to think what could have happened if you'd pulled over the wrong person? You could have been shot."

"We didn't think of that, Elvis."

With that, he eased up on us. "I know you didn't. But that blue light is serious, guys."

Rick spoke again. "We won't do it again, Elvis. We promise."

I followed Rick's lead and said, "Yeah, never again." Then we told Elvis what we were doing.

He smiled. "Did you meet any girls?"

Rick replied, "No. They took one look at us and drove off."

"I can see why. You thought you were Starsky and Hutch, but you look like Starsky and Much."

We had a good laugh that day but learned an important lesson: it was easy to get into trouble when it came to the ladies. While my brothers and I were learning these lessons, Elvis was fighting his own battles along the very same lines.

Elvis was always known as a ladies' man. From his controversial, hip-shaking appearances on *The Ed Sullivan Show* in the late 1950s to the rumors and press attention about affairs that dogged him the latter part of his career, the topic of Elvis's sex appeal was never far from discussion in the public's mind.

Were some of the rumors and innuendos true? Yes. But you have to look at this aspect of Elvis's life in the right context. Much of what has been said and written over the years about Elvis's philandering has been overblown to the extent that it has in some ways defined who he was. This is not a fair way to look at anyone's life.

It wasn't as if Elvis had a different girlfriend in every city. He did have occasional girlfriends, but his relationships didn't last more than four or five years because he was concerned about common-law marriage. He did not want to put himself in danger of someone claiming they were married if they had been in a relationship for a long time. As a result, Elvis's relationships did not last very long, sometimes as short as a week or two, or maybe a few months.

For the most part, Elvis's girlfriends were movie stars in California, where he shot movies. It wasn't as if he picked up someone off the street and just started having a relationship. These usually started out as a friendship with a costar, and then it became something physical. He was cautious and never got involved with call girls and that sort of thing.

Sometimes Elvis would notice an attractive girl at a concert and ask that someone bring her back to his dressing room or hotel afterward. He would talk to her, and sometimes things would progress further, but not always. You would be surprised at the number of women who said, "I spent the night with Elvis and nothing happened. He read the Bible to me." Sometimes, all he wanted to do was talk with a total stranger who didn't want anything from him.

Even so, it is important to acknowledge that Elvis did have relationships with a lot of women. This is an area where Elvis struggled with his sin. He was a work in progress, like all of us.

It is easy to judge him for this aspect of his life. However, the average person has no idea what it was like in his shoes. He was famous, handsome, wealthy, and had an enormous amount of charisma. He had the whole world in the palm of his hand.

Everywhere he went, women were constantly throwing themselves at him. I can't even imagine the battle that must have been going on inside his head. How many men could stand up under that kind of pressure? In retrospect, it's a miracle that he showed as much restraint and self-control as he did.

As someone who was so open about his faith and shared the gospel through music in his concerts, he was probably under spiritual attack as well. Ephesians 6:12–13 says, "For our struggle is not against flesh and blood, but against the rulers, against the authorities, against the powers of this dark world and against the spiritual forces of evil in the heavenly realms. Therefore put on the full armor of God, so that when the day of evil comes, you may be able to stand your ground, and after you have done everything, to stand."

Just because you realize you have a weakness and ask for God's help doesn't mean you will be perfect. Elvis was not a perfect man, and he knew it. More than once, I heard him say, "I am not perfect. I'm far from it. There is no perfect human being except for Jesus."

As his brother, I have been asked about this issue my whole life. I feel a responsibility to set the record straight. Jesus warned us about judging others in Matthew 7:1–2: "Do not judge, or you too will be judged. For in the same way you judge others, you will be judged, and with the measure you use, it will be measured to you."

When anyone wants to judge Elvis, I challenge them to judge themselves by the same standard. He who is without sin, cast the first stone.

The battle against sexual temptation is nothing new. It seems especially difficult for people of faith who are famous or have positions of influence. Spiritual influence and temptation always seem to go hand in hand.

Augustine, who lived in the fourth and fifth centuries, famously wrote about his sorrow and regret for his sexual sins in his *Confessions*. The book was the first major autobiography written in the Western world and has given Christians hope and guidance for more than fifteen hundred years.

King David, who wrote nearly half the Psalms and was described as a man after God's own heart (1 Samuel 13:14), had an affair with a married woman named Bathsheba and committed murder to cover it up. Even so, David wrote, "My flesh and my heart may fail, but God is the strength of my heart and my portion forever" (Psalms 73:26). In many ways, Elvis was a modern-day King David: an immensely gifted yet imperfect man whom God used to touch people through music.

People of faith have always experienced "failures of the flesh" because they are mere mortals. All of us are drawn to sin of various kinds. Does that mean we should evaluate a man's life based on one area of failure? Does that erase all the good he did, all the ways he blessed people with his gifts?

Elvis didn't think so. On the back page of his Bible, he wrote, "To judge a man by his weakest link or deed is like judging the power of the ocean by one wave."

This area of Elvis's life has been explored in such detail by so many people that it's like beating a dead horse. That is one of the reasons I wrote this book: to balance out the discussion about Elvis and to show that he was a man of deep faith. The beauty and goodness he brought into the world through his life and music far outweigh his sins.

Elvis was a major celebrity, but we shouldn't put him on a pedestal.

He never wanted that. He would say, "Never look to any man, because he will fall short." Elvis never set out to be a spiritual leader. He only wanted to serve his fans and give glory to God.

When people bring up this issue of Elvis's affairs, I always ask them this: How would you like it if we rounded up a couple dozen people who knew every aspect of your personal life and had them talk to the media about all your shortcomings? No one would sign up for that, yet that was what Elvis lived every day.

No matter how great the sin, God forgives us if we ask him. The biggest liar and deceiver in the world is the devil. He wants you to believe that your sin and failure disqualify you from serving God and leading others to Jesus. That's not what the Bible teaches, and it's not what Elvis believed.

When I think of everything I am today, it's because of Elvis. He taught me how to live, how to love, how to pray. He taught me how to build a relationship with God. He taught me to put God first, and then everything else will follow.

I am my brother's keeper and proud of it. Elvis protected me my whole life, and he is no longer here to defend himself. So, I will fight for his legacy and speak up when I feel he is being slandered.

James 1:13–15 says, "When tempted, no one should say, 'God is tempting me.' For God cannot be tempted by evil, nor does he tempt anyone; but each person is tempted when they are dragged away by their own evil desire and enticed. Then, after desire has conceived, it gives birth to sin; and sin, when it is full-grown, gives birth to death." Near these verses in his Bible, Elvis wrote, "Every man can be tempted, with God by your side you can be saved."

There's no such thing as a perfect man. But I'll always be grateful that Elvis pointed me to the perfect grace of God.

SIXTEEN

IF THE LORD WASN'T WALKING BY MY SIDE

It may surprise you to learn that the Elvis you saw in the movies wasn't much different in real life. Here's a perfect example.

One day in 1968, my brothers and I were riding in a limo with Elvis and some of the other guys, with a few others in cars behind us. We had been horseback riding all day at Elvis's Circle G Ranch, just a few miles south of Memphis. We were all dressed up as cowboys from the day's activities.

As we crossed over the Tennessee state line, Elvis said he was hungry and wanted a hamburger. We saw a place called Lotta Burger and decided to stop. The driver asked, "Do you want to go through the drive-through, Elvis?"

He said, "No, let's go inside and eat."

We walked in, and the manager, Mr. Cooper, came to the counter. I went to high school with his daughter and introduced him to Elvis.

He was surprised to see Elvis and was thrilled to meet him. Then he showed us to a large table, where we took our seats and placed our order.

As we were sitting there, a man walked into the restaurant, approached the counter, and started yelling. Elvis looked over at him and said to us, "I guess he's had a little too much to drink." We laughed, but it was obvious the man was drunk. We continued with our conversation about the day and the fun we'd had riding horses.

Suddenly, the drunk man started cursing and yelling at Mr. Cooper. Elvis stood up, and so did Red and Sonny. Elvis motioned with his hand to sit down and said, "I'll handle this."

We all watched Elvis walk over to the man. He stood next to him and asked, "Is there a problem, sir?"

The man looked at Elvis and squinted his eyes, realizing who he was. Then he said, "You're Elvis Presley, aren't you?"

Elvis smiled. "Yes, sir, I am." He stuck out his hand to shake the man's hand.

The man looked at Elvis's hand and sneered, "Well, if it ain't Elvis (blank) Presley!" (He added a few expletives I won't repeat here.)

Elvis smiled and asked, "Is there a problem, sir?"

The man started yelling and cursing again. "Yeah, the service around here sucks!" He continued, "The manager says I have to wait until your order is done before I can get any food."

Elvis looked over at the manager and said, "Sir, let this man have his food first. We don't mind waiting, and I'll pay for it." He looked back at the man and said, "Is that okay with you, sir?"

The man looked back at Elvis. "I don't need your money, you (blank-blank)."

Elvis said, "Okay sir. Let's forget it, then."

He was about to walk away when the man said, "Don't walk away from me, you (blank-blank). I'm going to kick your (blank) right now."

The man took a swing at Elvis, who did an outward block and spun the man around. In one quick move, he grabbed the man by the back of his shirt with one hand, and with the other hand he grabbed him by his belt, then walked him outside to his car.

Then Elvis said something to him and walked back into the restaurant. We stood up and clapped our hands, then yelled, "Way to go, Elvis!" He just laughed as we took our seats again.

Mr. Cooper brought our food to us. "This is on me, Mr. Presley."

"Thank you, sir, but I'll pay for the food." Elvis said.

"But I'd like to repay you for what you did."

Elvis smiled. "For what? All I did was take out the trash."

That was classic Elvis. He was always trying to do the right thing and protect other people. I've never met anyone who embodied Romans 12:17–18 as much as Elvis did. It says, "Do not repay anyone evil for evil. Be careful to do what is right in the eyes of everyone. If it is possible, as far as it depends on you, live at peace with everyone."

Elvis had plenty of opportunities to repay other people for harm they had done to him, but it was not in his character to do so. Sometimes those threats came in the form of random strangers. Other times, they were right under his nose.

∽

People assume the rich and famous don't have problems. In truth, they have bigger problems—and sometimes problems of an entirely different kind—than the average person deals with on a daily basis.

One of the most pressing problems they have is knowing whether someone wants to stick with them because of what they have or because of who they are.

Elvis knew that Rick, David, and I weren't there for the paycheck. We didn't even know who he was when we came into his life. We were little kids and only knew him as our big brother, even though all the adults in our lives knew about Elvis.

But with most everyone else, he always had in the back of his mind, *Does this person love me for who I am? They only hear my records or see me in movies, but do they know and love the real person?* He never knew who was really being loyal to him and who was not.

Plenty of people over the years hung around Elvis to try and get something from him. I suppose that's inevitable with celebrities. But I remember one guy in particular who tried to use Elvis to get what he wanted. He was trying to play Elvis and Colonel Parker against each other. The Colonel didn't want Elvis riding motorcycles or doing anything else to endanger his career because the Colonel's livelihood depended on Elvis.

This guy wanted to basically be a spy for the Colonel and tell him what Elvis was doing, while also pretending to be friends with Elvis. It was a major breach of trust because people in the outside world didn't normally know what was going on at Graceland.

I was there the day Elvis found out what the guy was up to. He paid the guy off with $10,000 and said, "Don't ever come around here again. If you ever see me walking down the street, cross to the other side. I never knew you."

This was more than a business transaction, and more than an inconvenience. This hurt Elvis. He considered this guy to be just like Judas, trying to sell him out to someone else. It was doubly hurtful because Elvis had a strained relationship with Colonel Parker to begin with.

The Colonel always wanted more control. From the very first days he began managing Elvis's career, he wanted to have as much say as possible, in as many things as possible. Elvis had his regrets about this arrangement more than once.

One time, the two of us were driving around Memphis and passed by Sun Records on Union Avenue. In passing, I said, "That's where it all began." Elvis had made his first recording, "My Happiness," there in 1953, when he was just eighteen.

I was surprised when he responded, "I wonder what would have happened if I had listened to my mom." Elvis rarely talked about his mother, so my ears perked up and I asked, "What do you mean?"

He continued, "My mom never did like Colonel Parker. Sometimes I feel like I sold my soul to the devil."

When Elvis began his career, his manager was supposed to be Hank Snow, the country artist who had started his own agency. Snow had teamed up with the Colonel to create a new agency, and Elvis was supposed to sign with Snow. He was a Christian and had recorded some gospel music, and Elvis's parents were happy about this. But between the verbal agreement and the actual signing, the Colonel had changed the contract to ensure he was the sole manager of Elvis.

Most of the people in Elvis's circle expressed their dislike for the Colonel, particularly Vernon, who felt that he couldn't even talk to his own son when Parker was in town. To the Colonel's credit, he was vital for getting Elvis media exposure in the 1950s. However, as time went on, particularly after Elvis got out of the army, the Colonel's approach became more and more outdated.

Other than that, the main people who caused Elvis grief were some family members who would come around now and again, asking for a handout. They didn't have any interest in a relationship with Elvis. They would only come around when they needed something. "Hey Elvis, can you help me with this? Can you give me that?"

Because Elvis didn't have the heart to say no, he would help them. It was the same with the Colonel. Elvis felt an obligation to him for getting his career started, even though he knew the Colonel was taking advantage of him. But Elvis was loyal to a fault and preferred to avoid conflict whenever possible.

You could say Elvis's number one rival was himself. He was a perfectionist who always wanted to top himself, to do better.

As I noted earlier, he would never listen to a song he had recorded. One time in the 1970s, Elvis and I were talking about music, and I mentioned his early stuff. I said, "I really loved all that older stuff you did back in the fifties—you know, the stuff that changed the world."

He responded with a disinterested, "Yeah."

"What?" I couldn't believe he would shrug off his early music like that. It was the music that had given him his start.

"I don't listen to it."

"Why?"

"I can go back and do better. If you listen to the vocals, I sound like a teenager."

"But you *were* a teenager, Elvis."

"Yeah, but my voice has matured a lot since then."

It even got to the point later on, when he was doing concerts, where he would rush through the medley of his early songs, like "Hound Dog." He just didn't enjoy performing them. Elvis didn't think anybody forty years old should be doing those songs.

If Elvis were alive today and saw legacy acts like the Rolling Stones still performing the songs they recorded as very young men all those decades ago, he would probably have no part in it. He would say, "More power to ya," but that wasn't for him. He was trying to get away from that character he had created, the original rock 'n' roll rebel, and transform into a more mature performer.

As he reached his later thirties, and especially into his forties, Elvis had less and less interest in treading water and doing the same things over and over again. He wanted to keep expanding creatively as well as spiritually. With each passing year as he got older, I could see him growing closer to the Lord.

Anyone who spent time around Elvis knew that he relied on God for everything. It's where he got his strength. Elvis was so appreciative of what he had and what God had given him. He thanked God every day and constantly sought God's guidance through prayer and reading the Bible.

The Psalms were especially close to Elvis's heart. Perhaps that's not a coincidence, because King David was also a musician who had his share of battles and at times was discouraged. Elvis particularly liked Psalm 118. He had underlined verses 8–9, which say, "It is better to take refuge in the LORD than to trust in humans. It is better to take refuge in the LORD than to trust in princes."

At the bottom of that page in his Bible, Elvis wrote a note to himself: "Trust in the Lord not man." He knew that people—including him—were frail and fallible. But the only one he could ultimately trust was God.

Elvis was also drawn to Psalm 43, which has a similar theme:

Vindicate me, my God,
and plead my cause
against an unfaithful nation.
Rescue me from those who are
deceitful and wicked.
You are God my stronghold.
Why have you rejected me?
Why must I go about mourning,
oppressed by the enemy?
Send me your light and your faithful care,
let them lead me;
let them bring me to your holy mountain,
to the place where you dwell.

Then I will go to the altar of God,

to God, my joy and my delight.

I will praise you with the lyre,

O God, my God.

Why, my soul, are you downcast?

Why so disturbed within me?

Put your hope in God,

for I will yet praise him,

my Savior and my God.

Despite being a world-famous celebrity with wealth, talent, and looks far beyond what most people could ever imagine, he was no stranger to problems and frustrations. Sometimes they came from others, and sometimes they came from himself. In either case, he took refuge in God's Word, knowing that God was the lighthouse giving him guidance in uncertain times.

Maybe that is why he wrote a brief prayer at the top of this page near Psalm 43 in his Bible: "Lord send me light to guide me."

He didn't ask for God's guidance only for himself. He also wanted it for his country, which was going through tremendous upheaval in the 1960s and 1970s. Elvis was a true patriot who not only served in the Army—he also wanted the world to know how he felt about the greatest country on earth.

SEVENTEEN

AMERICA, THE BEAUTIFUL

We are living in a time of great change. That has always been the case, no matter what decade or century a person has lived in. But the pace of change seems to be getting faster with each passing decade, and America seems more divided than ever.

People often ask me how I feel about America. To answer that question, I have to go back in time and tell you how I was raised.

My birth father was a career military man. The first six years of my life, in the 1950s, were spent as an Army brat, moving around from place to place. That is where the seed of patriotism was planted in my heart.

Throughout the 1960s, up through 1977, Elvis was the main influence in my life. He was a true patriot. He loved this country with all his heart and soul.

I remember one particular discussion I had with him about America. He said, "We live in the greatest country in the world, Billy. It was founded on freedom for religious beliefs and for political beliefs, in that order.

Our forefathers worked hard and fought for this country. They made this country what it is today."

He thought for a moment, then added, "If it wasn't great, then why do people from all over the world want to come and live here? I'll tell you why—because we are one nation under God."

I asked, "Then why do I see all these people saying they don't like it here?"

Elvis chuckled. "If they really don't like it here, then why don't they leave? There are planes and ships leaving this country every day. Are those people leaving?"

"No, I see them almost every week saying the same thing over and over."

"That's because they know they can't go to any other country and say stupid stuff about that country without fear of being persecuted. Only in America can they get away with that. The sad thing, Billy, is this: many people died for them. They died to keep us free."

I sat there for a moment, taking in everything Elvis was talking about. The wheels were spinning in my head. Then I said, "The thing I don't understand is, most of these people are in college. They are supposed to be smart. Don't they read the history books?"

"I'm sure they have, but they've taken God out of the equation. When you do that, you lose everything."

He could see I was thinking hard about what he had just said. He smiled, then added, "That's why it's so important that your generation keeps God as the foundation of our great country, Billy. Never lose that."

For Elvis, God and country were two parts of an inseparable whole. He believed in the principles the apostle Paul taught in Romans 13:1–5:

Let everyone be subject to the governing authorities, for there is no authority except that which God has established. The authorities that exist have been established by God. Consequently, whoever rebels against the authority is rebelling against what God has instituted, and those who do so will bring judgment on themselves. For rulers hold no terror for those who do right, but for those who do wrong. Do you want to be free from fear of the one in authority? Then do what is right and you will be commended. For the one in authority is God's servant for your good. But if you do wrong, be afraid, for rulers do not bear the sword for no reason. They are God's servants, agents of wrath to bring punishment on the wrongdoer. Therefore, it is necessary to submit to the authorities, not only because of possible punishment but also as a matter of conscience.

As an eighteen-year-old, Elvis became "subject to the governing authorities" by registering for the draft, as any dutiful young man would have done. And he continued doing so even when he was targeted for the draft.

∽

It is easy to forget that Elvis was controversial during the first few years of his music career. By today's standards, his music is tame, but at that time his music was so different that older generations felt threatened by his new form of music. Some felt this "newfangled" music needed to go, even though he was doing gospel music in addition to his regular music. But they chose not to see that part and instead focused on the music they didn't like.

Elvis wasn't the first rock and roll musician, of course, but he was by far the most well-known. He was the one who brought it to the mainstream. Some conservative leaders even called him the Antichrist! A segment of society wanted him silenced because they felt he was a dangerous influence on young people.

On December 20, 1957, as he was enjoying the holidays at Graceland,

Elvis received his draft notice for a two-year commitment in the Army. Because of who he was, other branches of the military were interested in using Elvis in noncombat roles, such as recruiter or entertainer. However, he brushed those offers aside and still chose to serve as a regular soldier.

His fans sent thousands of letters to the Army, asking for Elvis to be released, but he loved his country and was determined to serve his full assignment. However, he requested and received a deferment so he could finish working on the movie *King Creole* before he officially entered the service a few months later to begin his basic training.

Once in a while, Elvis would share a story about his time in the service. This was one of my favorites. One day in the winter of 1970, Rick, David, and I were talking to Elvis and complaining about how cold it was. Elvis said, "This ain't cold. I'll tell you about cold.

"The coldest I've ever been was in Germany," he continued. "When I was in the Army, one of my jobs was to sit on a hilltop in my jeep and watch the other guard. He was on the border, on guard."

"Did anything ever happen?" I asked.

"No," Elvis said. "I would just sit there and watch a Russian guard, who was watching me." Elvis laughed and continued. "One night it was so cold, I thought he was going to freeze to death. Then I came up with an idea. I took out my poncho and placed it over myself and the jeep, then started the engine. The heat from the engine started to warm me up. But the next thing I knew, I was lying on the ground next to the jeep. I looked around to see if anyone had sneaked up on me and knocked me out. I walked around the jeep, but there weren't any footprints. Then I looked at the jeep and the poncho. I saw the poncho was covering the exhaust pipe, and I realized what had happened—carbon monoxide had filled my poncho and knocked me out. God was watching over me that night. If I hadn't fallen out of the jeep, I would have died on that hilltop."

We said, "Thank God he was watching out for you, Elvis!"

"Yeah, that was a close one for sure."

Other than that one incident, Elvis's time in the Army was largely uneventful. He never whined or complained about being in the service. One time I asked him what he thought about the whole experience. He said, "I went and served my time, and I'm proud I did. But I didn't like the reason for it."

"What do you mean, 'the reason'?" I asked.

"To get me out of the public eye. They thought I was the Antichrist, ruining the children with my music." Then he added, "If you look at my movies before I went into the Army, I was moving a little bit. But after I came out, I didn't move as much. They had the female lead do the dancing."

It's true. There is a difference in Elvis's performances between his pre-Army and post-Army movies. He wasn't a rock and roll rebel anymore. Many times, I heard Elvis use the phrase "they clipped my wings" when he talked about his time in the Army. Even though the Army had changed him, and he felt he was unfairly targeted for the draft, he continued to be a strong patriot and supporter of the United States.

Elvis didn't like to make statements with his music. He didn't want to include anything about politics, drugs, or otherwise controversial material. He felt that wasn't the purpose of music. He just wanted to make people feel good with his music and point them to God, that's all.

He wasn't pointing fingers at everyone doing that sort of thing, such as the Beatles. I wasn't heavily interested in the political or drug messages in music, but I did catch it now and then in songs like "Happiness Is a Warm Gun" or "Everybody's Got Something to Hide Except Me and My Monkey." Of course, neither me nor my brothers would play that kind of song in front of Elvis because we knew he would say, "What are you playing that for?"

He knew we liked the Beatles. He would say, "Billy, music is supposed to be for entertainment purposes. It's not to make any political statements or sway anybody into drugs."

Elvis was occasionally questioned about this, as he was in 1972 when he was performing at Madison Square Garden. A reporter asked him about his political views, and he gave the usual response: that he was just an entertainer. Anytime they asked him what he thought of other entertainers who were more outspoken about their political views, he would say, "If that's what they want to do, that's fine." Elvis may not have agreed with those artists, but he wasn't going to go public about it. He didn't believe in judging anybody. If you asked him personally, he would tell you what he thought, but he wouldn't broadcast it.

If you spent any time with Elvis, you knew how he felt. He was especially outraged when he heard about the stunt Jane Fonda had pulled. She was a vocal anti-war activist and decided to tour North Vietnam in 1972. During her visit to Hanoi, she was photographed sitting on top of an antiaircraft gun, appearing to send the message that she wanted to shoot down United States aircraft.

Elvis flat-out couldn't believe she had done that. Here was an actress who had grown up in America with a father who was a famous actor in his own right. It was a slap in the face to our country. Lots of young men had died in Vietnam for our freedom, and she had used that freedom to travel to the enemy's territory and ridicule our troops.

∞

In military terms, a "hawk" refers to someone who loves their country and is willing to fight for it. Some might refer to Elvis as a hawk, but he was really an eagle.

In fact, Elvis loved the symbol of the bald eagle because it represented freedom—freedom that came at a price, freedom that God had given to us to enjoy, freedom we must keep alive. Elvis believed in peace, but he also believed in defending your freedom.

I remember when the heavy sentiment against the Vietnam War

started. Lots of people were saying they didn't like America and wanted to leave. We would be watching the news and Elvis would say, "I'll buy your ticket out of here if you don't like it that much. Go try that in Russia and no one will probably see or hear from you again." It really bothered him that so many people had died for our freedom just so others could make a platform for themselves and talk about how bad our country is.

Elvis wore his patriotism on his sleeve, almost in a literal sense. He often wore a lapel flag made of diamonds, rubies, and sapphires. He said, "Do you think I wear this for decoration? No, I wear it because I respect America." He couldn't handle the flag burnings—to him, it was a direct affront to everything he stood for.

Even his famous jumpsuits featured patriotic colors and eagles on the front, back, and belt. It was easy to buy Christmas gifts for Elvis. He loved anything with a flag or eagle on it.

He also respected others who helped us maintain freedom. During that time, whenever you saw someone in uniform, they were most likely a Vietnam veteran. Elvis would always stop and talk to them, give them money, or in some cases, give them cars.

He would do the same thing every time he saw a police officer. The first thing he would say is, "Thank you." I do that myself now. When I see someone in a police or military uniform, I always say, "Thank you." I have tried to pick up where Elvis left off.

One day, toward the end of the Vietnam War, a few of us guys were talking with Elvis about it. Someone said, "Well, we didn't win that one."

Elvis objected, "Now wait a minute. All we're doing is just backing out. We didn't lose anything. We shouldn't have been there to begin with, but we were there, and now we're coming back."

The guy said, "Well, we haven't won *everything*."

Elvis asked, "Have you ever listened to the Pledge of Allegiance?"

"Yeah."

"What does it say? 'One nation under God.' As long as we're under God, we will always be number one."

I know some people believe that's a simplistic way of looking at the world, but it's what Elvis believed. He was not a complicated man. He felt that if we, as a country, honored God, he would in turn protect us and make us successful.

Elvis loved the 1970 movie *Patton*, starring George C. Scott in the title role. He could quote the entire opening speech word for word. More than anything else in that speech, these lines sum up Elvis's feelings about America:

When you were kids, you all admired the champion marble shooter, the fastest runner, the big-league ballplayers, the toughest boxers. Americans love a winner and will not tolerate a loser. Americans play to win all the time. Now, I wouldn't give a hoot in hell for a man who lost and laughed. That's why Americans have never lost and will never lose a war. Because the very thought of losing is hateful to Americans.[2]

As a red-blooded American, Elvis loved playing to win. But he was never content to sit on the sidelines. He saw a growing problem with the drug culture that threatened America's youth. One day, in December 1971, without giving anyone advance warning, he took a little road trip that ended in one of the strangest and most fascinating episodes of his career.

EIGHTEEN

RUN ON

The National Archives and Records Administration (NARA) is the official record-keeping agency of the United States. The federal government generates a vast number of documents and materials, but only a tiny percentage are deemed important enough to be kept on file permanently for legal or historical reasons.

Their collection contains nearly 50 million images of various kinds. Suppose you were to guess which photograph might be the most popular. In that case, you might select any number of pictures of historical importance: maybe an image of the moon landing, a portrait of Abraham Lincoln, or a photograph related to events such as World War II or 9/11.

If you guessed any of those, you would be wrong. One of the most-requested images in the National Archives is dated December 21, 1970. It shows Elvis Presley dressed in a purple velvet suit and large gold belt, shaking hands with President Richard Nixon in the Oval Office. It's such a simple image, but it represents so much of who Elvis was and what he stood for.

In late December 1970, we were all at Graceland. I heard a discussion taking place in the other room, and it wasn't pretty. Elvis and Priscilla were arguing about money. All of a sudden, I heard a door slam. I got up and asked someone what happened and they said, "Elvis is going for a ride." We didn't know what he was doing but later found out he had decided to get a badge from the Federal Bureau of Narcotics and Dangerous Drugs, a precursor to the modern Drug Enforcement Administration (DEA).

This sounds pretty crazy to the average person, but you have to understand this was completely normal for anyone in Elvis's world. We were used to Elvis deciding he was going to do something on a whim.

The most surprising thing was that Elvis went out on his own. He had not traveled by himself anywhere in a long time. When he got to the Memphis airport, he told the lady behind the counter that he didn't have his wallet with him, then asked if he could write an IOU for the ticket. Since he was Elvis, of course they agreed.

The trip was completely spur-of-the-moment, but Elvis had been thinking along these lines for a while. He loved to collect badges, and all the badges he had were real. He had no intention of using his new badge to bust people. Rather, it was the idea behind the badge, and the power of having one, that drew him. Around the same time, Elvis had also talked to David and me about becoming narcs, but the government agent who came to see Elvis told him, "Your brothers are a little too well-known in this town to be narcotics agents." This had all been on Elvis's mind, and for whatever reason, the argument with Priscilla had prompted him to head off to Washington, DC, to get the badge.

Once Elvis landed in DC and checked in at the Hotel Washington, he flew to LA to meet his friend Jerry Schilling and told him he also wanted to arrange for Sonny West, one of our guys in Memphis, to join them. Elvis and Jerry flew back to DC together. On the flight, Elvis met George Murphy, a senator from California, and told him about his desire to get a badge. Murphy suggested Elvis write a letter to the president offering to assist in the nationwide war against drugs.

Elvis proceeded to write a letter on American Airlines stationery.

Dear Mr. President,

First, I would like to introduce myself. I am Elvis Presley and admire you and have great respect for your office. I talked to Vice President Agnew in Palm Springs three weeks ago and expressed my concern for our country. The drug culture, the hippie elements, the SDS, Black Panthers, etc. do not consider me as their enemy or as they call it the establishment. I call it America and I love it. Sir, I can and will be of any service that I can to help the country out. I have no concern or motives other than helping the country out.

So I wish not to be given a title or an appointed position. I can and will do more good if I were made a Federal Agent at Large and I will help out by doing it my way through my communications with people of all ages. First and foremost, I am an entertainer, but all I need is the Federal credentials. I am on this plane with Senator George Murphy and we have been discussing the problems that our country is faced with.

Elvis concluded the letter with details about where he was staying and how the president could get in touch.

Many people don't realize how conservative Elvis was. They perceive him as a rock legend, which he was, but he also believed in law and order. He had once told me, "The Army will clip your wings like they did mine." Elvis felt he was "watered down" when he came out of the service. He no longer had the desire to buck the system.

One time he made a kidding remark to me when I asked him what he thought about being in the Army. He said, "Well, that's real rock and roll right there. Especially when you're in a tank." He didn't like rebellion, he loved this country, and he sincerely wanted to help stem the growing tide of illegal drug use.

When their red-eye flight landed, Elvis immediately directed his limo to the White House, where he handed his letter to the guards and asked for a meeting with the president.

Later that day, having not heard from the White House yet, Elvis visited the Federal Bureau of Narcotics and Dangerous Drugs headquarters in DC. He tried to persuade the deputy director to give him a badge, but he refused.

A little later, Jerry heard from the White House. The meeting was on. We'll probably never know the real reason Nixon agreed to meet with Elvis—Nixon was an enigma to begin with—but the president's approval ratings were not so great at this time. He was dealing with the Vietnam situation and probably thought if he could take some publicity photos with Elvis and give him a symbolic badge, that might help his public image.

When Elvis went to the White House, accompanied by Jerry and Sonny, they had to hand over any weapons to the Secret Service. It wasn't unusual for Elvis and the guys in his entourage to carry multiple guns on them at once. As a celebrity, Elvis knew he was a potential target. In the previous decade, he had lived through the assassinations of John F. Kennedy, his brother Robert F. Kennedy, and of course, Martin Luther King Jr. Elvis had no intentions of leaving himself vulnerable to some lunatic with a gun.

Elvis told me the story later on about what happened with the Secret Service. When they asked for his weapons, he reached into his boot and took off one gun, then reached under his arm for another one and handed it over as well.

Then he said, "I need to use the bathroom." One of the Secret Service guys went with him. As he was doing his business, the derringer he had tucked behind his belt buckle fell onto the floor. When Elvis finished, the agent said, "Can I have that one, too, please?"

"Oh yeah, I forgot about that one." He handed it to the agent.

The three of them were escorted into the Oval Office, where they met with Nixon for a while. Sonny later told me that Elvis made himself at home, going through the president's desk and acting like a kid in a candy store. He was excited to be there.

White House photographers took lots of pictures of Elvis and Nixon, including the iconic photo of the two shaking hands. Elvis emphasized to the president that he wanted to help reach the youth of America and stem the drug problem. He also took a little dig at the Beatles for promoting an "anti-American" spirit. And of course, he asked about getting the badge, which Nixon agreed to provide.

After Elvis received his badge, he looked around the Oval Office and noticed a painting of George Washington on the wall. He walked over to it, and Nixon joined him and remarked, "That's a nice painting, don't you think?"

Elvis replied, "Yes, sir, but he sure did dress funny."

President Nixon looked at Elvis. "They can say the same thing about you, Elvis."

Without blinking an eye, Elvis said, "Mr. President, you have your show to run, and I have mine."

Nixon smiled, then turned and walked away.

When Elvis told me this story, I started laughing. He said, "What's so funny?"

"Only you, Elvis, would talk to the president of the United States that way."

Elvis smiled. "I didn't think of it that way."

He respected the office but was never intimidated by anyone, including the president. It didn't matter who you were. You could be John Wayne or some other movie star, but it didn't matter. Elvis taught me that no one is better than you, and you're no better than anybody else. We're all the same.

Elvis didn't have any problem dropping in to see a president, governor, mayor, or anyone else in a high position. It didn't matter what city we visited. If there was a badge to be had, he would always ask, "Could I get one of those badges?" And people were usually honored that he asked and happy to oblige.

Elvis always saw himself as an entertainer, not some larger-than-life person who was better than everyone. He saw what he did as just a job, no different than the guy who was out there digging ditches. Elvis didn't believe in using his celebrity status to gain favors or be looked upon differently.

That being said, he was awfully proud of his federal badge when he returned to Graceland. He loved showing it off to everybody.

Why did Elvis really want the badge? Was it a publicity stunt? A desire to add another piece to his unique collection? A spur-of-the-moment game to see if he could pull off a meeting with the most powerful man in the world?

There were bits of all those things, but the truth of the matter is that Elvis loved symbols of power. And what better symbol of power than a law enforcement badge, especially from one of the most formidable agencies in the country?

I'll never forget when he told me one day, "All my heroes wear uniforms." Specifically, that meant police and military. At one time, he made sure that most of the people who worked for him were deputized.

We grew up with a huge respect for the law. Those are men and women who put their lives on the line for us every day. They don't usually get paid a lot, so one of the ways we compensate them is with our gratitude. Elvis had a "blue streak" and considered a police officer's badge to be the ultimate sign you were worthy of respect. And since he couldn't get an FBI badge, a drug enforcement agency badge was the next best thing. In many ways, it was the ultimate police badge.

In 1970, Elvis was selected to receive one of ten awards granted to "Ten Outstanding Young Men" by the Jaycees, a civic and leadership organization for young men ages eighteen to forty. He considered it a great honor. In his acceptance speech, he said, "I read comic books and I was the hero of the comic book. I saw movies and I was the hero in the movie." Elvis did not only aspire to be an entertainer—he wanted to be heroic. And he wanted to support the men and women in law enforcement who helped protect the country he loved so much.

∾

Heroes come in all shapes, sizes, and styles. But one of the most important things I learned from Elvis is that heroes put their faith into action. He could have used his celebrity status to focus only on himself. He could have spent all his time and attention trying to gain as much publicity, wealth, and power as possible. But he wanted to use his power for good.

It wasn't just a faceless, nameless crowd Elvis was trying to help. His greatest fear was that Rick, David, or I would get involved in drugs. He did everything in his power to try and keep us on the straight and narrow. And by trying to help us, he also helped a whole generation.

People have long recognized how Elvis brought beauty, goodness, and generosity to the world through his life and music. It was gratifying to see this recognized by President Trump on November 16, 2018, when Elvis was presented a posthumous Presidential Medal of Freedom at the White House.

This award is one of the highest awards given to civilians in the US. It honors people who have made "an especially meritorious contribution to the security or national interests of the United States, world peace, cultural or other significant public or private endeavors."[3] The medal features a golden star with an inset of thirteen gold stars on a blue enamel background, all set on top of a red enamel pentagon. Bald eagles made of gold, with their wings outstretched, are set between the points of the star.

Elvis would have loved it.

Unfortunately, no one on Elvis's side of the family was there at the White House to represent Elvis at the ceremony. I would have proudly done so if I had been asked. Nonetheless, I was proud to see Elvis receive such a distinguished award. More than that, I was proud, as I am every day, to call him my brother.

PART 3

THE GREATEST OF THESE IS LOVE

NINETEEN

HOW GREAT THOU ART

Why do larger-than-life people like Elvis do what they do? Why do they go through the difficult process of trying to build a career? Why live with the unpredictability of fame and success on a large scale? Why put yourself out there so people can criticize your every move? Why try to reinvent yourself every decade or so?

Every artist has their own answers. Elvis loved music. He loved the audiences. He loved performing. He loved his fans. He loved the opportunity to help others because he was in a privileged position.

But there was one overriding reason he did what he did. Elvis was a man on a mission. It wasn't about having a career or creating the next album, concert, or movie gig. He saw what he did as a spiritual calling.

The apostle Paul had a mission too. He laid it out in Romans 1:14–17:

> I am obligated both to Greeks and non-Greeks, both to the wise and the foolish. That is why I am so eager to preach the gospel also to you who are in Rome.
>
> For I am not ashamed of the gospel, because it is the power of God

that brings salvation to everyone who believes: first to the Jew, then to the Gentile. For in the gospel the righteousness of God is revealed—a righteousness that is by faith from first to last, just as it is written: "The righteous will live by faith."

Paul preached the gospel from every imaginable place in the ancient world. Sometimes his "stage" was a Jewish synagogue, a prison cell, a ship, or even Mars Hill in the city of Athens. Elvis shared the same mission of spreading God's love. But he chose to share it through music.

Elvis started doing live concerts again after his 1968 TV special on NBC (the '68 Comeback Special). That whole experience was an experiment to see if crowds would still respond to Elvis. And indeed they did! Soon afterward, Elvis booked a residency at the new Hilton in Las Vegas. He interspersed these residencies with concert tours around the country.

In 1973, Elvis performed his famous *Aloha from Hawaii* TV special and included "How Great Thou Art" in the set list. This was his way of showing he was a true believer. He recognized that his ministry was his music. It was the only way he knew to get his message out.

Evangelism has always been challenging for people of faith. Even in the earliest days of the church, not every person who heard the gospel became a believer. Nothing had changed in nearly two thousand years— some believed, and some wouldn't. Elvis knew he had a much better shot at sharing God's love through the art form of music.

Why music? Music touches the heart directly. It goes straight to the emotions and moves people in a way that a sermon or lesson never could. Elvis was committed to using this powerful tool to reach as many people as possible.

Elvis also wanted to avoid the judgmental attitudes he saw in so much of the Christian world. It's hard to step on anyone's toes or cast a judgmental attitude when you're singing about God's love and grace.

His job was to put the message out there. His audience's job was to decide to either accept or reject the message. The funny thing is that it was probably pretty hard for a nonbeliever to reject the message of God's love when they saw how much the gospel moved Elvis.

There was something different about him when he sang gospel songs. The gospel message had changed him. He wanted the same change for his audience. When you let God in, something miraculous happens in your heart.

Or as Elvis would say, "That's God knocking on your door. Are you going to answer it?"

∽

Although Elvis recorded numerous albums of gospel music, he didn't see the gospel message as only contained within traditional gospel songs. A lot of the songs he used were not gospel songs, but they contained a message of inspiration, encouragement, or spirituality. Songs such as "Why Me, Lord?" and "You Gave Me a Mountain" all contained important messages Elvis wanted to share. If you listen to them with an open heart and an open ear, you'll see these songs are talking about faith.

Elvis has sometimes been criticized for not writing his own songs. Many other artists of his era—indeed, most of the popular ones—wrote many if not all of their own music. Elvis's main gift was not in writing songs, but in recognizing and selecting amazing songs that aligned with his worldview and message. Then he would put his own spin on them, adding something special and unique in the process.

For example, his rendition of Simon and Garfunkel's "Bridge over Troubled Water" is very different from the original. Yet the message is the same: the singer is telling the listener to give him their troubles and woes. He will lay himself down to be their bridge so they can make it across in a time of trouble.

If you take a moment to listen to Elvis's version, it is obvious he wasn't faking it. He meant every word. He wanted to be like Jesus, getting people through a hard situation. His whole life was focused on helping people and sharing love. It was the perfect song for him.

These kinds of songs were not straight-up gospel songs. They were not necessarily written from a Christian viewpoint. However, Elvis turned them around and used them to express his love and faith. He wanted to get people focused on the Lord. Sometimes you have to do that in indirect ways.

∽

Gospel wasn't just a style of music Elvis incorporated into his concerts or used to fulfill his recording contracts. It was also his heart language and a way to unwind after the emotional high of a concert.

When Elvis came off the stage, he would be so wound up with energy that it was impossible to turn it off. He never gave a half-hearted performance. Even if he felt something could be musically a little better, or he was unhappy with some small aspect of a concert, he never gave anything less than 100 percent of his energy.

Giving out all this energy affected him. You would think he would be exhausted, but it was the exact opposite. All the love and affection he had just put out to the audience was now coming back to him, and it filled him.

The only way he knew how to come down from this high was to sing gospel. Elvis would gather with some people in his hotel suite, usually with the gospel quartet that accompanied him onstage, and one of the guys from the band would sit down at the piano and get started. Because Elvis would be there for weeks at a time, he would have the hotel bring in a piano during his stay there. Elvis was bringing in a massive amount of money for them, so they would do whatever he asked.

They would sing gospel songs until the sun came up or until Elvis said, "I'm ready to go to bed." They would sit up there for hours, and people would come up after the show. It was almost like a second concert. After the midnight show, Elvis would invite people up and they would go on for hours. People would stand around and listen or they would mingle in the suite.

One of the songs I heard frequently in these postconcert settings was "Lighthouse." In an unusual move, Elvis chose not to be the main singer. He did add some vocals, but his background vocalist Donnie Sumner sang the lead. If you watch the documentary *Elvis: That's the Way It Is*, you'll see Elvis and the group singing "Lighthouse."

There is a fascinating story from 1 Samuel 16 that tells how King Saul was being tormented by an evil spirit the Lord had allowed to come upon him. Unbeknownst to Saul, young David had been anointed as the next king, and it was only a matter of time before he would replace Saul.

Ironically, David was also in the service of King Saul. One of Saul's servants had heard about David's ability to play the lyre, and had recruited David to perform for the king. First Samuel 16:23 says, "Whenever the spirit from God came on Saul, David would take up his lyre and play. Then relief would come to Saul; he would feel better, and the evil spirit would leave him."

This story reminds me of the power of music to soothe and comfort in all kinds of circumstances. For Elvis, gospel music played much the same role. He took refuge and found comfort in this sacred music, long after the lights of the stage had faded and into the wee hours of the morning.

TWENTY

AMAZING GRACE

If you do an analysis of any artist's catalog, you will find a core message. Most artists focus on relationships, because it's a topic that dominates our lives. Turn on the radio or listen to the past few decades' worth of pop, country, or rock music, and you will mainly hear songs about love, loss, getting together, and breaking up.

Elvis had plenty of these kinds of songs too. But that was only part of the story. His gospel music selections showed that his hope for his fans was that they would believe in God with all their hearts and souls.

He had the faith of a child. He didn't believe in making things complicated. I remember Elvis saying, "Just because you can't hear or see something doesn't mean it's not there. You can feel the wind, but you can't see it. It's the same with God. He's there, and even though you can't see him, you can feel him. If you just respond to him, you will see it." That's why Elvis used music to help people not just *hear* the words of the message but *feel* it.

Elvis was always revealing a lot about his life and what he was going through with a song. He was very transparent with his fans, even though some people never caught on and couldn't see what he was trying to do.

This was a new thing for performers. If you think back to the beginning of the entertainment industry, vaudeville performers, music performers, and radio and TV stars had little interest in being transparent. It was all about entertainment. It was all about putting on a show, and in the case of radio and TV, bringing in advertising dollars.

But Elvis wanted to do more than entertain. Did he put on a fantastic show? Yes! But within that entertaining show was also a transparent message to his fans: "I need God's grace, and so do you." You didn't have to read in the newspaper what was happening in Elvis's life. You just had to listen to the songs.

Once Elvis made a note to himself on some stationery from his home:

Philosophy for a Happy Life: Some[one] to love, something to look forward to, and something to do!

He believed that you needed God in your life to provide all those things. And he trusted God to give those things to him.

Many people just saw the glitz and glamour. They just heard upbeat songs that made them dance or sing. They didn't sit back and listen carefully to the words he was singing.

When Elvis sang, he was pointing you to the question, but he was also giving you the answer. He is the most transparent man I ever knew. He didn't pull any punches. He was sharing his life through songs.

Once I went to Elvis and asked, "How do you show someone you care about them?"

He said, "When words fall short, say it with a song."

There is a common thread you hear from Elvis fans. You can pick up this thread if you talk to someone who went to one of his live shows. You can also see it if you look at many of the comments on YouTube underneath Elvis's concert videos, among other places. The comments go something like this:

- "There will never be another artist as good as Elvis."
- "Elvis was the greatest entertainer ever."
- "Nobody can match the passion and vocals of Elvis."

What are these people trying to say? They are saying there was something extra, something unique, something one-of-a-kind about Elvis that no one else ever had.

These fans realize that with Elvis, it was more than a show. They could see he was opening his heart and sharing it with the world. I hope that when people read this book, they will look at his music a different way. I hope I will have given them a glimpse of why Elvis did what he did, and how that explains the difference that came through in his performances.

Ultimately, that's what Elvis wanted—for you to see that he was different and to hear the message he was trying to convey.

His biggest concern was that most people were missing his message. He was worried that all they saw was this energetic, eccentric guy onstage, shaking, singing, and doing his thing. Which is fine, but that's missing the point. He wanted you to know what was happening in his life, and how it could help save your life . . . especially your eternal life.

If you watch a video of Elvis singing the gospel song "Oh Happy Day," you will see what I mean. You can see during the song when the Holy Spirit touched him. There's no denying it.

This is a big contrast to other artists who had "a great voice and great technique, but had no heart," as Elvis would put it. He would say, "If you can't put your heart and soul into something when you're singing, then don't even bother."

This is what fans are getting at when they say no one will ever top Elvis. He had the voice, the flair, the technique . . . but above all, he had the heart.

In Matthew 25, Jesus told a story about a master who had three servants. He entrusted his wealth to them while he was away on a trip. He gave the first one five bags of gold, the second one two bags, and the third servant one bag.

The master was gone for a long time on his trip. When he returned, he asked for an accounting of his gold. The first two servants had both doubled their investments. The master was pleased with them and entrusted them with even more.

However, the third servant had hidden his bag of gold in the ground. The master scolded him and took away what little he had.

God gave Elvis an almost unlimited amount of gold. And Elvis felt responsible for using the gifts God had given him to serve people and honor God. As a result, he had an incredible impact on his listeners, who not only enjoyed great music, but heard a life-changing message as well.

～〇〇～

Earlier in the book, I talked about Elvis wanting to get back to doing live performances. This was his true passion. As much as he enjoyed being in the studio and making movies, what excited him most was getting in front of a live audience, giving them his love and energy, and feeling their energy in return. Nothing excited him more.

But why did he enjoy that process so much? Certainly because it was fun, but there was something more—he had an urgent message to share. It was important to him. There was something about being in a room with a crowd and singing about the gospel that he couldn't replicate in a recording and he could never do in a movie. Elvis was totally in his element when he was onstage.

How many times have you ever been to a rock concert, and then suddenly the performer throws a couple of gospel songs into the middle? Probably never. But when you saw Elvis in concert, especially from the early 1970s onward, you can bet that's what you would get. He was going to let you know where he stood because God had given him the talent and the message to do it.

It sounds so simple, and in this cynical day and age, maybe even simplistic. But the fundamental truth is that Elvis wanted you to know that God loves you. He wanted you to pick up the Bible and believe in God because he wanted to see you in heaven. That's how convicted he was.

As I mentioned before, Elvis was the same person onstage and off. There was no difference. This was especially true in how he talked about God.

Elvis was not one to "chapter and verse" anyone. He didn't like to throw the Bible in people's faces or be obnoxious with his message, the way so many Christians like to evangelize. Rather, Elvis would simply talk about how great God's love was for us all, and the sacrifice Jesus had made on our behalf.

Toward the end of his life, he talked to evangelists such as Rex Humbard and Oral Roberts about the gospel message. He recommitted his life to God and was saved again because he didn't want to have any doubt about his eternity.

It was kind of a funny thing, and also serious in a way, but one time in Las Vegas, he was talking to Sammy Davis Jr. Sammy noticed Elvis wearing both a Star of David and a cross necklace—two things that don't normally go together because they represent two distinct religions: Judaism and Christianity.

Sammy said, "Elvis, isn't that kind of a contradiction?"

Elvis looked at him and said, "I don't want to miss heaven on a technicality."

He wanted to do everything in his power to ensure he went to heaven. That's where he wanted to go. It was the most important thing in his life. Family was important. Music was important. His career was important. But first and foremost was his relationship with God and his eternal destiny.

Nothing mattered to Elvis more than making sure others were there too.

The gospel is what helped Elvis get through hard times. It was his lifeline to God. In John 16:33, Jesus told his disciples, "I have told you these things, so that in me you may have peace. In this world you will have trouble. But take heart! I have overcome the world." Elvis took comfort in God's strength and peace to help us in difficult times.

That is why Elvis loved the song "You Gave Me a Mountain." It was the idea that God has given us something hard to do, but he has also given us the strength to overcome it.

He once told me, "You're going to go through hard times. Everybody does. And after you have gone through it, that means God has given you a new strength and another hurdle you don't have to face anymore. And if it does come back up, you know what to do. Be thankful for even the hard times you went through in life, because you learned something. God is going to get you through it."

Elvis taught me that we can talk to God about our problems. Why do we so often just talk to friends about our difficulties, when God is the One who can get us through? He doesn't give us anything we can't handle.

Even when we grieve somebody we have lost, we can take comfort that they are much happier as they watch over us. We selfishly want them to stay with us for as long as possible. It doesn't mean we shouldn't grieve for that person now. It just means they are in a better place and are not suffering.

Gospel music is what made Elvis tick. He said, "If you listen to gospel music, it's just like listening to somebody singing the Bible." It was the only music he would sing around the house. There were many times that he would be sitting in the piano room, playing a gospel song, and I would walk by.

One time, not long after we moved into Graceland, I heard Elvis playing the piano and I walked in to ask what he was playing. He said it was gospel music. I said, "That sounds great, Elvis. But this doesn't sound like the music on your records." By that time, I had gotten familiar with the music he was recording for his movies.

He said, "That's because my heart is in this, Billy. That's what I do for a living, but this is what I live for."

A few decades later, in 2001, Elvis was posthumously inducted into the Gospel Music Association's Hall of Fame for his contribution to the genre.

Elvis would have appreciated it, but he didn't live for awards. His greatest reward was getting to share the gospel message in front of thousands of fans every night. Nothing brought him more joy.

But with the opportunity to share the gospel in front of thousands of people also came the unique burdens of being a superstar. Sometimes this took the form of problems from former friends and associates. Sometimes it came from the pressure of having a huge fan base. But the most intense pressure came from himself.

TWENTY-ONE

HELP ME

If you toured Graceland in the 1980s or 1990s, you might remember a gold record with a broken glass cover. There is a funny story behind that.

One day in 1970, Elvis, Rick, David, and I were sitting in the den together. Vernon walked in with a new gold record. We all looked at it and congratulated Elvis on his new gold record. Vernon left, and as we were talking, a thought came to me. I asked, "Elvis, is that really your record, or is it made to look like a record?"

Elvis said, "Good question, Billy. Let's see." Then he picked up a large ashtray and was about to break the glass.

We said, "Whoa, Elvis! Don't break the glass! It's not that important." I continued, "I was just wondering what's on the record, that's all."

Elvis said, "All these years, and I still don't know what's on any of them. So, I'm going to find out today."

We all said, "Okay," and he broke the glass. He took it out of the case and we walked downstairs with him to the basement to play the record. He was all smiles and having a great time.

He dropped the needle on the record—and we heard Slim Whitman! Slim was a country music artist who had toured with Elvis as his opening act in the 1950s. Rick, David, and I busted out laughing as Elvis stood there with a funny look on his face. Then he started laughing also.

We took the record off the stereo and Elvis said, "I can't believe RCA would give me a gold record with Slim Whitman on it. I wonder what's on the others?"

We laughed and told Elvis, "Let's not find out."

That story is a perfect analogy of Elvis's life. From the outside looking in, it appeared that Elvis had a perfect life. He was talented, handsome, and wealthy. Although he enjoyed those blessings and used them to honor God, he also dealt with a lot of temptations and pressures that are unique to someone at his level. One of the most heartbreaking pressures you can possibly face is when you are betrayed by those closest to you.

∞

As any celebrity knows, the people who work for or around you know all sorts of details and stories they can later use to expose details of your private life. Many times, this is not done with the best of intentions.

In early 1977, Red and Sonny West, along with Dave Hebler, a bodyguard, published an exposé titled *Elvis: What Happened?* They had all previously worked for Elvis and claimed the book was an attempt to help get Elvis back on track. I thought that publishing a book with all sorts of horrible details and stories about someone's life was an awfully strange way of helping someone.

Elvis was hurt and surprised by the book. They claimed to be his friends, and then they published a book like that just for the money. That's not friendship. That's revenge.

I talked to Sonny on the phone shortly after Elvis passed away. I told him it was a "Judas act," an act of betrayal. He didn't see it that way.

In all fairness, everyone makes mistakes. I'm not sure if they would have published the book if they could go back and relive that period. We have to learn to forgive people for the hurt they have caused us. And that's exactly what Elvis did. He had a very Christlike attitude about it. Elvis forgave those guys for what they had done before he passed away later that year.

It wasn't easy for him, but he knew that things like that would happen sometimes. People you think are your loyal friends will sometimes stab you in the back.

As the world's first superstar, Elvis just took it all in stride and didn't get hung up on what people did to him. He didn't keep emotional score-cards on other people or himself. Whenever the topic of mistakes or regrets would come up, he would sometimes quote the line from Frank Sinatra's "My Way": "Regrets, I've had a few, but then again, too few to mention."[4]

Elvis knew he made mistakes. We all do. But he was a class act, quick to love and quick to forgive.

The public, however, did not always do the same. They expected Elvis to maintain a certain image that became harder and harder to uphold as the years went on.

∞

During a 1972 press conference at Madison Square Garden, one of the reporters asked, "Are you satisfied with the image you've established?"

Elvis said, "Well, the image is one thing and the human being is another, you know."

The reporter followed up. "How close does it come? How close does the image come to the man?"

Elvis replied, "It's very hard to live up to an image. I'll put it that way."

Americans have always expected their celebrities to be slim, trim, and fit. In recent years, we have become a more accepting culture, but this wasn't the case in Elvis's time. Occasionally there would be a celebrity who was a little more rotund, but this was always played to comedic effect, as in the case of actors such as Jackie Gleason.

Elvis liked to eat. He was an ordinary southern boy who liked banana pudding, mashed potatoes, and the works. He maintained a slim figure until the 1970s, when he put on a noticeable amount of weight. As he got older, it was harder and harder to stay at the same weight he had been when making movies. It was a constant battle for him the last few years of his life, when things were made more complicated by a host of other health problems. It was impossible to live up to that image of perfection.

If you want a sense of the pressure a celebrity is under, take a look at all the well-known people over the years whose careers have gone downhill because the public got a glimpse of an imperfect life. Whether it's their appearance, drug use, legal problems, or some other crisis, the worst thing you can do is show any weakness. In America, we like our celebrities perfect.

Elvis gets a lot of credit for being the first rock star, which by definition is associated with rebellion. It's the whole sex, drugs, and rock and roll image. He caused an uproar with his dance moves onstage because they were much more sensual than people were used to seeing on television.

However, Elvis made a point to emphasize that he was very much an all-American boy who loved mom and apple pie as well. That's why he insisted on singing "Peace in the Valley" on *The Ed Sullivan Show* in 1957, even though it was totally unexpected to do a gospel song on that program. His mother, Gladys, loved that song, and it was his way to honor her as well as God. Elvis was trying to let people know, "I'm not who you think I am."

Elvis and I once discussed the pressures and temptations of fame. He said, "Billy, everybody faces a daily battle of right and wrong. You constantly have to make decisions, and those will determine what happens to you. What kind of person are you going to be?"

Then he hit me with a challenge. "Always try to be good."

It wasn't until after his death, or shortly before, that all the negative stuff started coming out about him. He wondered not only what his fans would think, but what his daughter would think as well. He hated to let people down. He wasn't a healthy person at that point, and the grief and stress certainly didn't help.

That's why he was constantly praying and asking God for wisdom. Elvis knew the devil was after him. But he would also say, "The devil's after everybody, you know." He didn't single himself out as someone who was uniquely tempted. He knew everyone faced temptation and struggles. I'll never forget the advice he gave me about how to handle it.

One day in 1972, Elvis and I were watching something on TV about the Vietnam War. We weren't talking, just watching the program. Before it ended, he said, "Did you know there's a battle going on inside everyone?"

"You mean between good and evil?"

"You are close. But, there's another one that people don't see or really think about."

"Really? What is it?"

Elvis thought for a moment. Then he said, "Before I tell you, let's look at a few things first. The brain is amazing in everything it can do. It can control everything the body requires. It controls our thoughts, it helps us talk, and it helps us process what we see and what we hear."

"Yeah, it does." I wasn't sure where he was going with this.

"But everyone overlooks the heart, Billy."

I gave him a curious look. "What do you mean, Elvis?"

He said, "When you see someone from a foreign country, or even someone from here, what do you see?"

I chuckled. "It depends on where they are from, I guess."

"Wrong answer, Billy."

This got me even more curious. I asked, "Well, what do *you* see, Elvis?"

"I see a human being. There are no colors, just people."

"Oh yeah, I know about the colors, because you taught me that a long time ago."

He smiled, then said, "Most people don't open their hearts to see people, or hear what they say, or really talk to them."

I was slowly catching on to what he was saying. "I think I'm beginning to understand."

"What are you thinking with, Billy? Your brain or your heart?"

Then it dawned on me and I smiled.

He said, "Now you're getting it, Billy, because your heart expressed your thought."

"Wow, Elvis!"

He continued. "The heart is capable of doing everything the brain does, but the heart will never lie to you. The brain will. It tells you that it's the most important thing in your body, but it's not. The heart is. Everything good comes from the heart. For example, love, kindness, mercy, hope, and forgiveness all come from the heart."

I said, "I never thought of it that way."

He smiled again, then asked, "You know why you haven't?"

"No."

"Because you haven't learned to open your heart and let it handle things."

I asked, "Well, it seems pretty simple to me. Why doesn't everyone do this?"

He said, "Because they are afraid of being hurt. What they don't know is, that's what the brain is telling you—to be afraid, don't trust this person, or don't listen to that person."

Elvis's advice was so simple I just sat there in awe. I said, "Wow! I'm going to try and live this way from now on, Elvis."

"Your brain just told you to try, and your heart told you, you will. It takes practice, Billy. It's something you have to work on every day."

"I will, Elvis. I will."

"You've heard the old boxing expression, 'Lead with your left,'" he said, "or if you're left-handed, 'Lead with your right'"?

"Yeah."

"I'm telling you to lead with your heart, Billy. Lead with your heart."

In the years since I had that conversation with Elvis, I've always tried to lead with my heart. I had no way of knowing at the time that Elvis was not only struggling to lead with his heart, but he was also facing a lot of changes, both in his career and his personal life.

TWENTY-TWO

FARTHER ALONG

In the last few years of his life, Elvis was coming into a time when he had experienced all the success he could possibly hope for. He had reached the pinnacle of the entertainment industry. He had performed concerts for hundreds of thousands of fans in countless venues, starred in lots of movies, made boatloads of money, dated beautiful women, driven fast cars, and had everything he wanted at his disposal.

Yet there was a discontent, a desire to do more. It wasn't a desire to be more famous. It was a hunger to draw closer to God.

At this stage of their career, most performers want to keep achieving more and more. They want to keep climbing higher. But Elvis wanted to go deeper—deeper in his faith, his understanding of God, and his ability to change people's lives with the gospel.

By the mid-1970s, I wasn't working for Elvis anymore. However, I was still in the loop of the happenings within Graceland. I saw Elvis and the rest of the guys frequently. We could all see he was going through transitions.

Elvis had gotten saved again. In evangelical terms, this meant he had rededicated his life to God.

When you see photos or videos of Elvis performing during this period, you see a flashy guy in a white jumpsuit, full of energy and wooing the screaming fans. But Elvis was so much more than that. He was full of contradictions. The casual observer would never guess that he had a deepening walk with the Lord and a seriousness that did not often come through his music. Elvis was seeking the deep things of God and never turned down the opportunity to talk with pastors or spiritual leaders.

The apostle Paul wrote of his own struggle in Philippians 3:7–14.

But whatever were gains to me I now consider loss for the sake of Christ. What is more, I consider everything a loss because of the surpassing worth of knowing Christ Jesus my Lord, for whose sake I have lost all things. I consider them garbage, that I may gain Christ and be found in him, not having a righteousness of my own that comes from the law, but that which is through faith in Christ—the righteousness that comes from God on the basis of faith. I want to know Christ—yes, to know the power of his resurrection and participation in his sufferings, becoming like him in his death, and so, somehow, attaining to the resurrection from the dead.

Not that I have already obtained all this, or have already arrived at my goal, but I press on to take hold of that for which Christ Jesus took hold of me. Brothers and sisters, I do not consider myself yet to have taken hold of it. But one thing I do: Forgetting what is behind and straining toward what is ahead, I press on toward the goal to win the prize for which God has called me heavenward in Christ Jesus.

Whenever I read this passage, I think of Elvis. He and Paul were not so unlike each other. They may have lived in different times and cultures, but they both dealt with health problems, they wanted to know Christ more deeply, they faced struggles and frustrations . . . but ultimately, they kept pressing onward because of the gospel message they wanted to share.

∽

Those of us who knew Elvis best could sense that changes were coming. Sometimes Elvis kept his intentions to his inner circle, but other times he made his intentions clear to the whole world, like when he would announce that he was trying to line up an overseas tour.

Elvis had always set his sights on doing a European tour. He had served in the Army in Germany for a couple of years. But this time, he wanted to return as a performer, not a soldier. He even had Lamar Fike, one of his close friends, look into getting another plane, since they wouldn't allow the *Lisa Marie*, his personal jet, in Europe because of emissions regulations.

Colonel Parker was the main obstacle to organizing an international tour. By this time, he was pretty much a hack—a "carny" as they say—and that's all he was. In the 1950s and early 1960s, he might have been able to pull off something truly spectacular. But after Elvis's movie career wrapped up in 1969, Elvis wanted to get back where he'd wanted to be all along—onstage in front of his fans. He wanted to tour Europe and Asia. The Colonel's solution was, "Let's do a satellite special."

Don't get me wrong. Lots of people saw Elvis's special *Aloha from Hawaii via Satellite* in 1973, but it was just a stepping-stone to what he really wanted to do. It's one thing to be on television, but it's entirely different being in front of thousands of people in a live concert. Elvis lived for his fans and wanted to be standing in front of them all around the world.

He was grateful for the residency at the Hilton in Las Vegas. But his question was, "Why do people have to travel to Vegas to see me? Why can't I just travel to see them?" That's the way he put it.

Fortunately, Elvis had the help of Jerry Weintraub, a concert promoter and later a film producer who had come up through the ranks due to the Colonel's mentoring. Although the Colonel had basically made Jerry's career by giving him a shot and showing him the ropes, the Colonel was the one now needing help to take Elvis's career to the next level.

Jerry had been the concert promoter for Elvis's national tours but now wanted to suggest something more. One time he approached Elvis while the Colonel was standing there. Jerry said, "What if I told you I could put you in Wembley Stadium, ten nights in a row, a million dollars a night?

Elvis said, "You can do that?"

The Colonel objected to Jerry's suggestion and said, "You'll have to pay me off."

Jerry said, "That's no problem."

This surprised and scared the Colonel. Maybe he wasn't as vital to Elvis's success as he used to be. The Colonel didn't realize that Elvis was not planning on keeping him around. He had become more of a liability than an asset.

I don't know how many more people Elvis was going to let go, but he wanted me to come back and work for him. I wasn't aware these behind-the-scenes changes were happening while I was gone. In fact, I wasn't aware of it until Elvis passed away. But at the time, it really threw me when he said, "There are going to be a lot of major changes."

I didn't ask him what he meant by that specifically. I trusted that he knew what was best. It was always important for me to be there for people who needed me, especially Elvis. That's who I learned it from. He taught me to be a loyal friend and supporter to people close to you.

Maybe that's why Elvis had such a hard time letting go of the Colonel after all those years. The Colonel had given Elvis his big break. If it wasn't for the Colonel's marketing savvy and promotion, especially in the early years, Elvis's career might have looked a lot different. And if Elvis had lived longer, he might have gotten to do one or more international tours like he wanted.

But in that moment, Elvis had to decide how strong those bonds of loyalty should remain when it came to business. At the same time, he was also looking to his family to be loyal in carrying on his legacy in the event something should happen to him.

∞

About a month before he passed away, Elvis called Rick, David, and me up to his bedroom. Whenever he called the three of us to his room, we had a little routine we would follow.

"What did you do wrong this time?"

"I didn't do anything!"

"Look what you've done now!"

We assumed somebody must have done something wrong because he wanted all three of us. I was confused because I hadn't done anything, and neither had the other two.

When we got to Elvis's room, he was sitting on the edge of his bed with some paperwork in front of him. The Bible was sitting open in his room also. Whenever you entered his room, you could always see he had been reading it. We all sat cross-legged on the floor in front of the bed.

Elvis said, "You've heard your mom and Daddy are going to get a divorce, right?"

We said, "Well, not really." The news didn't come as a complete shock because we had heard rumblings, but we didn't know things were getting to the stage of being official. Again, we had grown up in the age of "children are meant to be seen and not heard," and even though I was in my early twenties by this time, Vernon and Mom didn't talk to us about those kinds of private matters between them.

He said, "Yeah, it's going to happen. I just want to know what you're going to do."

The three of us looked at each other. We had no idea what he meant. I wasn't working for him at the time, so I wasn't sure what he was talking about.

Then it dawned on me. Elvis wanted to know if we were going to stay part of the family. So, I said, "Elvis, that's just them. That's got nothing to do with us, does it?"

He said, "I'm glad to hear you say that. You're right. It's between those two and doesn't have anything to do with the four of us."

Rick, David, and I agreed. "We're not going anywhere, Elvis."

Elvis was so relieved to hear it. He reiterated that the divorce was a separation between Vernon and our mom and did not affect the relationship the three of us had with him.

Then Elvis got a bit emotional. He said, "If anything ever happens to me, you three will be the ones to tell my story."

That shocked us. I said, "But Elvis, you have Billy Smith and lots of others to tell your story. They've been with you a lot longer." Billy was Elvis's first cousin. They had grown up together in Tupelo, Mississippi, and later moved into Graceland when Billy's father started working for Elvis as a guard.

Elvis said, "But nobody can tell my story from a brother's perspective like you three can."

He wasn't only concerned about his future legacy. He was worried about it here and now, as well with the publication of *Elvis: What Happened?* earlier that year. As I said before, former bodyguards and confidants Red West, Sonny West, and Dave Hebler had claimed they'd written the book to help Elvis, but it was a hatchet job, plain and simple. The book was an unfair representation of who Elvis was.

Elvis talked about the book and how much it hurt him. From the average person's vantage point, it may seem like celebrity tell-all books don't have any impact on a famous person. They have fame and fortune, so why would they care what others say about them?

This book hit Elvis on a deep level. I believe the stress and anxiety it caused him probably contributed to his emotional and physical decline those last few months. It put him in a dark place because he was worried how it would affect not just his legacy but his relationship with his daughter.

That's why Elvis wanted us to be the ones to tell his story. He wanted people to hear the truth.

His mood was muted that day, not just because of the topic, but because he wasn't feeling well. When Elvis felt good, it was always a happy conversation. But when he wasn't feeling well or would be in a funk, he would talk about death and linger on questions about what would happen to him.

The three of us picked up on that. We were so in tune with him we could immediately sense his mood and then respond. When he said he was worried about something happening to him, we knew we had to turn things around and get him to see the good.

We said, "Elvis, nothing's going to happen to you. You'll probably outlive us all. You're going to be sitting up here at Graceland with your grandkids, having a great time." He laughed at that.

Then David stood up and pushed Elvis on the shoulder. "Well, you're not going anywhere without your number one guy!" David was his personal bodyguard at the time.

Elvis replied, "What—you think you can handle me?"

David said, "You bet! Stand up and I'll show you."

Rick and I got up immediately because we could see this was heading toward one of our epic wrestling matches. Elvis looked at the three of us. "You three think you can do this?"

We said, "Yeah, come on!"

"Well, bring it, buddy!"

We had succeeded in changing the mood pretty quickly. We were eager to get Elvis to a happier mindset and didn't want to linger on morose topics. Had we known that just a few weeks later, Elvis would be gone, we would have had a much longer conversation about his real legacy and how he wanted us to keep it alive.

On his 1967 gospel album *How Great Thou Art*, Elvis recorded a song titled "Farther Along." The lyrics express the singer's hope that although life is filled with temptations and frustrations, God has a bigger plan and they will understand things better "farther along."

Something in Elvis's demeanor that day, as well as our conversation, told us that he was farther along his journey than any of us realized. But like the apostle Paul, he kept pressing on toward the goal.

He wasn't going to stop for anything.

TWENTY-THREE

KNOWN ONLY TO HIM

Once Elvis told us a story about filming his 1967 movie *Easy Come, Easy Go.* He played a Navy frogman who spends his life deep-sea diving, singing at a nightclub, and of course, chasing women.

Elvis was taking a break while filming a scene on the water. He had taken off his scuba tank and mask but left his weight belt on. He was sitting on the side of the boat, listening to everyone talk about the next scene, when suddenly, a wave hit the side of the boat. It knocked him out of the boat into the ocean.

He tried to swim, but the weight belt pulled him under. He was sinking fast and tried to remove the belt but couldn't see the release latch because it was too dark underwater.

As Elvis sank deeper, he started to panic. The wave had hit them by surprise and he didn't have time to take a deep breath before going overboard. He had no idea how far he had sunk.

Finally, he found the latch, the belt came off, and he began to swim up. It seemed like an eternity as he swam to the surface. He thought for sure he was dead as he started having convulsions from lack of air.

He told himself, "This is it." Suddenly, there was air and light as he popped through to the surface. Elvis said, "The first thing I did was thank God."

When he finished telling us this story, we said, "God was with you that day, Elvis."

He smiled at us. "Yes, he was."

Elvis was no stranger to the topic of death. Numerous people in his family had died young. He wanted to help me and my brothers understand that death is just a passage to the other side.

One time a friend of mine passed away and Elvis paid for the funeral. He said, "Billy, it's okay to miss your friend. But you've got to know this: he is now in a far better place than we are right now. So don't fear death."

Anytime someone passed away, that is the first thing he would say: "They are in a far, far better place than we are right now. If anything, you should be rejoicing for them." It was his way of comforting me whenever someone passed away.

Most people have a fearful attitude toward death and the afterlife, but Elvis and the Presley family looked at it differently.

One night in 1960, Vernon and I were watching *The Late, Late Show* on TV in the kitchen at Graceland when I thought I heard footsteps upstairs. It was strange because Elvis wasn't there. He was off making a movie at the time.

I asked Vernon, "Did you hear that?"

He said, "No."

I didn't say anything and continued watching the movie. I heard the footsteps again, so I asked Vernon again, "Did you hear that?"

He looked at me. "What did you hear?"

"It sounds like someone is upstairs. I can hear them walking around."

"No, I didn't hear anything." We continued watching the movie, but a few minutes later I heard them again. This time, Vernon heard it too.

He turned the TV off and said, "It's time for bed." His reaction left me a little confused, but I didn't question him.

A month or so later, Elvis came home. My brothers and I were playing with him in the backyard. When we got tired, we took a seat and he asked how things were when he wasn't home.

That's when I told him what had happened that night. He looked at me and smiled, then said, "Let me show y'all something." He put David on his shoulders, took Rick and me by the hands, and we walked into the house. We went upstairs to the attic.

We had never been in the attic before. When we walked in, we saw an old electric train, a lot of old clothes, and Elvis's army footlocker. Elvis took David off his shoulders and we walked over to the train. He said, "My mom bought this for me when I first started making a lot of money. She knew I always wanted one when I was young."

We looked at the train set for a moment, then walked over to the footlocker. Elvis said, "This was from my Army days." He opened it up and showed us his Army clothes.

Then we walked over to the old clothes. Elvis said, "These are my momma's clothes. I couldn't stand the thought of giving them away, so I kept them." Then he said, "What you heard that night, Billy, was my momma. Ghosts aren't like what you see in movies. Sometimes they come back to watch over you and warn you of the dangers ahead."

My brothers and I looked at each other and then at Elvis. We didn't know what to say. Elvis sensed we were uneasy and said, "Never be afraid. My momma would never do anything to harm you. She was only watching over you like she does me."

After he said that, we all smiled. Throughout the years at Graceland, we all heard strange noises and footsteps but took comfort in what Elvis had told us. We were never scared when we heard the sounds because we knew who it was and what she was doing.

Elvis always seemed to have a particular sensitivity and interest in matters of death and the afterlife. Maybe this was because he sensed his life would be unnaturally short.

Elvis rarely talked about death directly, but he hinted that he thought he wasn't destined for a long life. Sometimes he would see Vernon coming or going around the house, and Elvis would comment, "Yeah, there goes the Silver Fox. He's going to outlive us all."

It wasn't a morbid thing that Elvis thought he would die early. A lot of it came down to genetics. The Smith side of his family—his mother's side—had a history of people dying tragically young. His mother died when she was only forty-two, the same age Elvis was when he passed away.

Regardless of how short or long his life was, Elvis intended to live every moment. He would say, "My time here is short. That's why I live every day like it's my last."

Once I asked him, "What does that mean?"

"The Smith side of the family, a lot of them passed away young."

"But that doesn't mean it's going to happen to you."

"Thank you for saying that, but I think otherwise."

When I was around twelve, I remember Elvis taking me to visit the morgue. I don't remember why we were there, but I was naturally a little freaked-out by the dead body we saw. Elvis said, "Don't look at this. It's just a vessel. His spirit has gone on to heaven. What you see on the outside, the body, is a temple, and you must take care of it, but it's just a vessel to get us to the other side."

Elvis was just like anyone else. He was a great entertainer, but he was also a human being, with feelings. Growing up, he saw things, with people dying young, that really affected him. Those things stayed with him, and he wondered how long he would be on this earth.

That's why he taught me that life is a gift from God. We should thank God for that every day. When we're gone, we're gone. There is no encore, so we have to do what we can do while we're here on this earth.

This is why Elvis operated the way he did. He gave everything he had. The last time we talked, on August 14, 1977, he was still trying to teach me.

∞

My final conversation with Elvis began with a question: "Billy, do you believe God forgives you for your sins?"

This question threw me, because he had been teaching me the Bible for seventeen years. We'd had countless discussions about God, Jesus, faith, and so many other related topics. Where was this coming from?

We had been messing around with a karate knife when Elvis accidentally hit me with it, giving me a blood blister. He was freaking out over it, which was unusual for such a minor injury.

We were standing in front of the sink in the bathroom. He asked the question about God forgiving my sins, and I looked directly at him in the mirror. I was perplexed.

I said, "Yes, of course, Elvis."

"Good. That's what I wanted to hear you say. You know, we've all done things that probably weren't pleasing to God. We should all be asking for forgiveness."

I stood there wondering where this was going. I said, "I pretty much do it every day."

"I'm glad to hear that."

We talked more about God's grace and how it's the only way to get to heaven. Then he reflected on his own struggles with womanizing. "I pray for that. I pray for the strength to stop. I knew I was doing wrong, but I never lost my faith."

It was rare for Elvis to be this vulnerable about his shortcomings. "The devil will approach you and say, 'You did this or that, and you're not going to have God's grace.' But that's a lie. The devil is the biggest liar in the world. Don't listen to him. He can hit anybody at any time. Here's what's great, though: if you feel guilty, and you know you've done wrong and prayed about it, that's when the Lord has touched you."

He continued, "What separates right from wrong is when you know that you've done wrong and you won't try to do it again."

Elvis never did stop with women, but that was his weakness. Every human's got them, and that was his Achilles' heel. Elvis always said, "I don't want anybody to try to be like me." What he meant was that he wasn't perfect. He was human, just like everybody else. Despite having so many raving fans, it bothered him that all they could see was what was onstage. They didn't know what was inside his heart.

This was an unusually reflective conversation, so I tried to change the subject to sports, but he interrupted me. "You know, I really love you."

I said, "I love you, too, Elvis," hoping to change the subject. But he kept at it. He stayed in that serious mood for a while. It felt uncomfortable that he was talking to me that way. I'm not sure why. I'd had that discussion with him when others, like Rick and David, were around, but this was different. I'd never had this kind of serious one-on-one talk with him. Plus, I couldn't figure out where it was coming from.

I tried to change the subject again. "Well, what do you think the Packers are going to do this year? Or how about the Cleveland Browns?"

He looked at me, disinterested. "I don't know." He paused. "I just really wanted to let you know how I feel about you." Then he began to talk about what was coming. "There are going to be a lot of drastic changes. I'm going to be getting rid of some people, and I would really like to have you back with me, man."

"Elvis, you've got Rick and David. You don't really need me."

"But if I asked you to come back, would you?"

"You know I would. Elvis, I'll do anything for you."

"That's what I wanted to hear."

The conversation lingered on a variety of topics for well over an hour. Then I asked a question that had been on my mind for a while. "Elvis, do you think I'll ever find love?"

"What do you mean?"

"When girls see me, the first thing they say is, 'Oh, that's Elvis's brother.' Do they date me because of who I'm related to, or do they want to know the real person?"

He smiled a bit and said, "Now you know what I've been through." For years, Elvis struggled to find women who were interested in more than just his public image.

"I know it's been tough on you."

"Yes, it has been. Billy, whenever you go looking for love, you'll never find it. It will hit you when you least expect it. And when it happens, it will turn your whole world upside down. You'll wonder where they have been your whole life and how you ever got along without them." Then Elvis added a warning. "And when you find it, don't mess it up like I did."

"What do you mean?"

"I was in love twice." I was about to say one of those must have been Priscilla, but he said, "It's not who you think it is. You'd never guess."

I was curious to hear more but didn't pursue it any further. He continued, "Love is something that when it happens to you, your whole world will change. It will turn upside down. You'll never be the same afterward when you find true love."

A little later, our conversation turned to my plans for the future. Elvis said, "There's one thing you should never do, Billy."

"What's that?"

"Never give up on your hopes and dreams."

"You know I like to race." Elvis knew about my love for cars and racing. We had spent countless hours over the years riding together and getting into mischief now and then.

"One day it will happen. It may not be what you expect. But somehow you will be associated with it. So never give up on that."

The conversation started to wind down when he said, "I love you, Billy." I just smiled at him because I had no idea that was the last time I'd see him. He gave me a hug and I patted him on the back.

Elvis was a little misty-eyed. We looked at each other in the mirror and changed the subject, like guys often do after a vulnerable moment. He joked, "Well, what do you think the Browns are doing today?"

We laughed. I said, "I guess my finger's going to be okay. No big deal."

"All right. So, am I going to see you on the sixteenth?"

"Yeah, I'm supposed to help Rick and David." I was going to help them load for the upcoming tour. I would always come over and help drive some of the guys to the airport for a tour.

As I was walking down the stairs, he said, "Okay, I'll see you on the sixteenth."

"Okay, Elvis."

Driving home, it dawned on me. *You didn't say you loved him, Billy.* I hit the brakes and slid over to the side of the road. *Maybe I should go back and say it.* I was dumbfounded and had no idea where this impulse was coming from. I thought for a moment and decided, *No, you'll see him on the sixteenth.*

I wish I had listened to my heart. I wish I had gone back.

∞

Rarely has a week gone by when I haven't thought about that conversation. It upsets me when I think about him telling me, "I love you," yet I didn't respond. I just patted him on the back. He knew how much I cared about him, but I didn't say the words.

I'm not afraid to tell people how I feel about them anymore. I tell my wife, Liz, every day. I don't know how many times a day she hears me say, "I love you." When I talk to my family, I tell them. I let them know.

Elvis taught me one of the most valuable lessons of my life: there is no guarantee of tomorrow. As Psalms 90:10–12 says:

> Our days may come to seventy years,
> or eighty, if our strength endures;
> yet the best of them are but trouble and sorrow,
> for they quickly pass, and we fly away.
> If only we knew the power of your anger!
> Your wrath is as great as the fear that is your due.
> Teach us to number our days,
> that we may gain a heart of wisdom.

Once again, Elvis was a step ahead of everyone. He sensed that the sun was setting low on his life. But nobody knew that in three days' time he would be gone.

TWENTY-FOUR

IF WE NEVER
MEET AGAIN

August 16, 1977, began like any typical warm summer day in Memphis. I got up and went to Bailey Aircraft, where I was an assistant jet mechanic. I had already made plans to get off work early to help Rick and David pack for the upcoming tour. We were also going to throw them a going-away party. I was excited about helping and couldn't wait to see them.

I was also looking forward to seeing Elvis because I couldn't stop thinking about the last conversation I'd had with him, two days earlier. I wanted to tell him, "If you need me, I'll be there."

I hopped in the car and turned up the 8-track. But before I headed to Graceland, I stopped by a store with a few of my friends. They walked back to the manager's office because they knew him. I lingered back to grab a Coke and some items for the party.

When I walked back to the manager's office, there was an awkward silence. I thought, *Why are they looking at me like this?* Then someone said, "We just heard on the radio that Elvis is dead."

I said, "Hey guys, don't kid around. That's not funny."

It took a couple more attempts for them to convince me they weren't kidding. They told me I needed to call Graceland. A woman answered, but I couldn't tell who it was. All I said was, "This is Billy. Is it true what I heard on the radio?"

The woman was crying and said, "Yes. You need to get up here as fast as you can."

I dropped the phone and the guys said, "We've gotta get you to your car." They helped me out to the parking lot, and I put my hand on the car door. I dropped to my knees and looked to the sky. "Why, God, why?" I hung my head and started to cry. A million things ran through my head, one of which was, *If I had been there, maybe I could have done something.*

I regained my composure and got in the car. I wasn't in any state to drive, but somehow I made it to Graceland. There was a large crowd when I got there. The police moved the crowd so I could drive up to the gates. As I drove through the gates, I remembered the first time I had done so in 1960. I drove to the backyard and saw Rick and David standing outside. I got out of the car and walked over to them, and no one spoke. We just hugged and began to cry.

I saw Lisa Marie driving her golf cart toward us. She came to a stop beside me and asked, "Uncle Billy, do you want to take a ride with me?"

I said, "Not right now, Sweetie, but I will later." As she drove off, I asked Rick and David if she knew what had happened. They said yes. I now wish that I'd taken that ride with her.

∽

We weren't the only ones caught in the nightmare. Everyone in the family was hurting too. Elvis had been our older brother and a father figure as well, but Vernon was understandably having an especially hard time coming to grips with what had happened.

Things were not always smooth sailing with Vernon. But Elvis was his son and his world. He had nothing else to live for.

On August 16, I thought there would be two deaths—Elvis and Vernon. As I stood there talking with Rick and David, I asked, "Where's Daddy?" They told me he was sitting in the kitchen, so I went in to talk with him. I wanted to see how he was doing and hoped I could comfort him in some way.

He was sitting in a chair that someone had pushed away from the counter. I had never heard that kind of moaning and weeping before. It sounded like a broken soul, which I'm sure he was. I walked up and knelt down in front of him. He put his hand on my shoulder, then said, "He's gone, Billy. Sonny's gone."

"I know, Daddy. He's in heaven now."

Vernon then tried to stand up, and I helped him the best I could. Once he was up, he hugged me. I could feel his body shaking uncontrollably. I held him tight because I thought he was about to fall. All he could say was, "He's gone, Billy. My Sonny's gone."

I started praying as we stood there. *Please, God, be with Daddy. Don't let him die today.*

One of the maids came up to us and said, "Maybe he should sit down, Billy." I agreed and told Vernon he should sit down. He didn't want to let go at first, but I said, "I'm not going anywhere, Daddy. I'll stay with you if you want me to."

"Please do, son." When I heard him call me "son," I broke down crying with him. I eased him back in the chair and knelt down beside him, putting my arm on his shoulder.

He looked over at me. I reassured him, "I'm not going anywhere, Daddy. I'll stay as long as you want me to."

I knelt there with him for about thirty minutes. I watched him as people would come in the house and try to talk to him. I didn't say anything, but people told me, "I'm glad you're with him, Billy."

The phone rang, and one of the maids answered it. She said, "Dr. Nick will be here shortly."

I stood up. "Daddy, I'm going outside for a while. If you need me, send someone to get me, okay?"

"I will, Billy. Thank you."

I walked outside not knowing this would be the final time I was with Vernon. It was the last real talk we would ever have.

The sights and sounds of that day still haunt me sometimes. I've replayed the days after the funeral in my head over and over again. How can someone go from having a family to having nothing that fast? But I've learned to accept that's the way Vernon was. No matter how he saw it, I still loved him. I always will.

∞

In the years since Elvis passed, there has been lots of speculation about what he might have achieved if he had lived longer. I can speculate that he may have wanted to get more into dramatic roles, maybe even directing films. I know for sure he was interested in doing a European tour.

But maybe there is a sense in which the speculation doesn't matter—not because we wanted Elvis to leave, but because he had completed his mission. Yes, there are health reasons Elvis left this world. I can also tell you Elvis was a man who rose to the occasion when faced with challenges. He was a man with a mission. He had done what he had set out to accomplish.

There could have been more albums, more concerts, and more creative endeavors. But Elvis gave his heart and soul to his fans, everything he had, for more than two decades. Maybe he just needed to rest.

Elvis never stopped striving to top himself. He loved his fans so much that he didn't know what it meant to take a break. When he died, he simply didn't have any more left to give.

If you opened Elvis's Bible, you would see a note he had written to himself under Psalm 46, quoting verse 10: "Be still and know that I am God." Elvis had talent, charisma, fame, and fortune, but he struggled with stillness. Now that his journey was over, I hoped that he found the rest that always seemed to be just out of reach.

Elvis often talked about the afterlife. He would say, "If I die before you, I will do everything I can to show it's real. I'll send a message somehow."

I always dismissed this conversation because it was so morbid. At his funeral, as his casket was being placed in the hearse, a huge tree limb broke off and hit the ground with a loud thud. The tree was in good health, and it wasn't windy. There wasn't an explanation for why the tree limb fell. As we were riding in the funeral procession, I thought of what Elvis had said. I took it as a sign that there was an afterlife and he was happy.

I wish I could have said the same for me. His death hit me hard, and I felt like I was on an elevator, riding it to the bottom floor of life. It would be ten years before I heard from Elvis again.

TWENTY-FIVE

SEEING IS BELIEVING

My brothers and I responded very differently to Elvis's death. Ricky immediately turned his life around. He went to seminary in Dallas and became a pastor. A year or two later, David became an evangelist. I was the rebellious one who went the opposite direction.

I don't believe God was punishing me for my bad decisions. I just didn't know how to grieve. As a result, I turned to drugs and alcohol. I became the prodigal son who hadn't come home yet. I was acting out and behaving badly but still believed in God.

The only ray of light during this period was Liz. We had met shortly after Elvis's passing, and I fell for her before we even said hello. It happened exactly like Elvis told me. He had said, "Whenever you go looking for love, you'll never find it. It will hit you when you least expect it."

Liz was the first woman I dated who never cared about my connection to Elvis. She liked me for who I was, not for what I could get her, or the opportunity to be around a celebrity. We dated for a couple of years, but I just couldn't bear the thought of taking her down the destructive path I had chosen for myself. So, we broke up.

Around 1980, three years after Elvis passed, I was still in Memphis. My brother Rick had moved away but had come back home to visit. We were sitting on my mom's balcony, having a conversation. He didn't like where my life was headed, and he made no bones about it. I was slowly killing myself.

Rick began talking about God's love and how Jesus had died for our sins. I felt convicted because I had been baptized when I was fourteen, but I had never really understood the meaning of it. We talked about Elvis and how he had rededicated his life to the Lord before he passed away. Rick also told me about Elvis's conversations with a few of his spiritual mentors.

"Do you think you're ready?" he asked me.

"Rick, I really need help right now. I don't know what I'm doing."

"That's why you've got to turn this over to God."

"Rick, I've tried."

"You tried, as in . . . did you do it? Did you actually turn your life over to God?"

"No."

As we talked more about God's love and Jesus' sacrifice, I felt convicted. I said, "Rick, I want to get baptized."

"Why don't we do it now?"

Rick and I started walking down to the swimming pool. My mom lived in an apartment complex. On the way down there, he started kidding with me. "I'm going to dunk you twice just to make sure God takes away the stuff you've done." He was making me laugh, which was classic Rick.

Rick baptized me, and for a little while I felt clean, renewed, like my life was on a new pathway. But as soon as he left Memphis, I went back to my old ways. However, I knew God was still with me even though I was using drugs again.

Rick and David had both been big influences on me. It was a big shock when I went down to Texas a few years after Elvis's death and both of them were preaching. I was impressed. Suddenly, I was the one who was on the outside looking in, seeing the changes in their lives.

When I visited their churches, I would just sit there crying like a baby because I was convicted. Elvis had mentioned several times that destiny had brought us all together. Rick said, "Whenever you decide to share your testimony, Billy, it's going to be a very powerful one."

I didn't know what he meant by that.

He continued, "You've got to remember this. God has given us a key."

"What do you mean?"

"What are we going to do with that key? Are we going to try and help save lives? Like Elvis would want us to? Or are we going to act like idiots, like you've been doing?"

I started to feel convicted. But the conviction wasn't enough to pull me out. I needed something more.

Fast-forward to 1987, ten years after Elvis passed. By that time I was living in Nashville and had spent a decade wandering in the wilderness, like Moses. I had also gotten married in 1984 and my daughter, Brooke, was born the same year.

I had heard that people on the other side of death sometimes try to communicate with you through dreams. One night I had been drinking and using drugs pretty hard. When I fell asleep, I had a dream I was talking to Elvis, and I asked, "What does it feel like to be dead?"

He gave me a blank stare. "Don't you know?"

I woke up immediately and knew that my lifestyle had to stop. I couldn't go this direction any further. I knew I was going to die if I kept living like this.

The next day, I asked my mom to help me. She took me to a drug treatment center. When I talked to the people there, they recommended I do an outpatient program. But I told them if I did that, I knew that as soon as I got out of that meeting, I would use again. They said they usually did a thirty-day treatment, but I ended up staying there forty-five days in inpatient care. That's how bad I had gotten.

During the program, I discovered what I had been doing to myself. I was running away from my problems. The clinic staff warned me that just because I stopped using drugs, my problems wouldn't disappear. But at least now I knew how to deal with them instead of trying to avoid them.

My first real test came before I even left rehab. My wife had sent divorce papers and moved with our daughter to San Diego, where I had spent some time after Elvis passed away.

When I got out of rehab, I moved to Florida. Rick had been kind enough to buy me a bus ticket and put me up in a trailer. I started to attend AA meetings, sometimes going as many as three or four times a week. I also started attending church and was fortunate that my trailer just happened to be next door to a church Rick attended. Rick was a traveling evangelist, but it was his home church.

My involvement in AA helped me to see where I needed to make amends and get every area of my life back on track. I was willing to do anything to get my daughter back, even if it meant getting back together with her mother.

My mind went back to a time when I was eighteen and I was sitting in the basement at Graceland with some of my friends. Lisa Marie was there with us also. By this time, Elvis and Priscilla were divorced, so Lisa Marie was just visiting. She asked me to play and I said, "No, I'm going to be with my friends for a while."

As she was walking away, a thought came to me. *If you ever have children, they will always know who their daddy is.* I wasn't close to my birth father, and Priscilla only got to spend nine years of her life with Elvis. Lisa Marie didn't really know her own father, since Elvis died when she was very young. So, I promised myself that I would do whatever it took to be a part of my daughter, Brooke's, life.

As a result, I moved to San Diego to be near her. I knew in my heart that Brooke's mom and I weren't meant for each other, so I focused on taking care of Brooke. Her mother and I made a brief reconciliation, and a friend of mine asked if I would be interested in writing a book about my life with Elvis, so I agreed.

Our little family moved to Nashville, but the writing of *Elvis, My Brother* put a strain on our marriage. When the book was released in 1989, we went our separate ways, but I was awarded custody of Brooke.

After our separation, I had a few relationships, none of which lasted very long. Then I was introduced to someone. I wasn't sure if she was "the one" or if I was just settling for what I thought would be a good environment for Brooke. We dated for a while, then got married, but the relationship did not last. We divorced soon after Brooke moved to be with her mom.

At this point, though, I was happy with my life. Or I should say, I was happy with what I was doing. I had become a Harley-Davidson salesman, and I wasn't in a relationship with anyone. I was living with my mom because of her health problems, which had sadly taken a turn for the worse.

One day she called me at work and asked me to take her to the ER. For the next several months, I watched her slowly deteriorate. Mom's wish for many years was to see all three of her sons together at one time. Two days before she passed away, she got her wish. Rick, David, and I were all with her when she took her last breath.

Shortly after I lost my mother, I got a call. I hadn't heard Liz's voice since 1979, when we broke up, but I knew who it was right away. During that time I had been married and divorced, and also dated other women.

But I had never stopped thinking about her. From the moment we broke up, I did my best to find somebody like her. I was always searching for someone with dark hair and brown eyes, but I never found her. There was only one Liz, and I missed her deeply.

When we reconnected and talked for several hours, I took this as a sign from God. I said, "I've got it this time, God." During the two saddest times of my life, God gave me Liz to comfort me.

I asked Liz if I could come to Memphis to see her. I needed to see if those feelings that I had years ago, and continued to have since I met her, were still there. I made plans to drive from Nashville to see her. The weather was terrible that night—I even drove through a tornado in Brownsville, Tennessee! But nothing was going to stop me from seeing Liz again. When we saw each other, it was like we'd never been apart. We spent the rest of the night crying and talking about the things that happened to us over the years.

Life with Liz was fantastic. I moved back to Memphis, and we attended church weekly. We built our relationship around God, and he became our foundation. My life seemed settled in a way it had never been.

But everything changed on May 19, 2018.

People have all sorts of responses to what I'm about to share with you. But I can tell you for sure that this was my experience. I'm not prone to crazy thinking or dramatic stories. After all, I'm a mechanic who solves problems with logic and reason. You are free to believe or not believe. All I can do is share what I have seen and heard.

It was an ordinary Saturday, nothing unusual. Liz and I were at her daughter Ashley's house. Her other daughter, Emily, was there also. I had to run a few errands and came back to the house around noon. I was tired and not feeling well.

My brother David was with me, and I asked if he'd like to watch a movie. He was a little hesitant but finally agreed. We went upstairs, where I turned on a movie and lay back on the couch. A couple of minutes into the movie, I began to feel a little sleepy. What I saw next changed my life.

I was standing above what looked like clouds. It was very bright, but I couldn't see the source of the light. The light surrounded me and illuminated everything I could see. I saw what looked like a city off to the right. It was far away and had a gold hue to it. It was different from any city I had ever seen. The city itself was glowing, and I could make out the tops of a few buildings, as well as steeples.

Upon seeing the city, something inside me said, *That is where you are supposed to go.* I looked down at the clouds and wondered if they would hold me up. I took one small step, and it was solid beneath my feet. As soon as I took that first step, I immediately felt an overwhelming sense of love. I use the word *love*, but words can't describe how strong that sensation of love was. It's like the first time you ever fell in love, magnified a million times.

I usually walk fast and am sort of an anxious person, but I felt totally at peace. I walked slowly and was not in a hurry because there was no sense of time. All the worries you feel in your everyday life are not present in heaven. You just feel a euphoric sense of love, joy, and peace.

As I was walking toward the city, I noticed a crowd of people. I had never seen that many people before. I couldn't make out who they were. All I could see were their silhouettes. Everyone was dressed in white, and what separated them from one another was the color of their heads. I was dressed in white also. It looked like a robe and was the brightest shade of white I had ever seen.

Then I saw a figure standing in the distance. The sensation of love became ever more intense. I didn't know who the figure was at first, but when I got closer, he turned around. It was Elvis. I was happy to see him, and he was happy to see me. He didn't have to say it. I could sense it. The wonderful thing about heaven is that you don't have to use your mouth to speak. You can hear the other person's thoughts.

"Billy." Elvis smiled and looked directly at me.

"Elvis." I took a step toward him.

He stepped forward and gave me a hug. Then he pushed me back a little and looked at me. He said, "It's good to see you." As soon as he said that, it was as if the edges of my vision grew darker and started to close in on Elvis's face. I started to get scared because all of a sudden, the darkness started to move toward his face.

He said, "Tell all of my family, friends, and fans I love them. And I'll see them when they get here. I love you, Billy."

"I love you too." I finally got to say the words I wished I'd said thirty-one years earlier, after our final conversation.

Then a voice spoke to me. It was the most commanding yet calming voice I'd ever heard. I knew it was God. He said, "No doubt, no fear, Billy." When God talks to you, he doesn't have to explain anything. I knew exactly what he meant: "Don't doubt there is a heaven, and have no fear. This is where you're going to go if you believe with all your heart and soul that Jesus came and died for you."

As the darkness surrounded me, I heard another voice. It was Liz screaming, "Don't leave me! Please don't leave me!"

∽

I opened my eyes and saw Liz above me. I asked, "What's going on? Why am I lying on the floor?" Then I saw the paramedics coming up the stairs. I asked again, "What's going on?"

The paramedics put me on a gurney. They said, "Don't worry, son. We'll take care of you. You'll be at the hospital in no time." They put IVs in me, and I slowly calmed down.

After I arrived at the hospital and was lying in the ER, Liz and David started telling me what had happened. David said, "You died, Billy."

I said, "What?"

Liz said, "Yes, baby, you died."

I asked, "How long was I dead?"

Liz and David talked between themselves to get the answer. Then they said I was gone about ten or twelve minutes, maybe a minute or two longer. I didn't say anything. They continued telling me what had happened.

David said, "I thought you were snoring, but then I looked over. You were jerking around, and white stuff was coming out of your mouth. I didn't know what to do, so I ran downstairs and got Liz."

Then Liz said, "When I came upstairs, you were still foaming at the mouth. Then your whole body stiffened up and you went limp. Your eyes were open and dilated. Ashley and Emily came running upstairs. Emily called 911, then Ashley started doing CPR on you. We told 911 that the CPR wasn't working. The people at 911 asked if you were still on the couch. We said yes, and 911 told us to put you on the floor and try again." Liz had single-handedly pulled me off the couch, then Ashley continued the CPR. After a few attempts, I came to.

That's when a nurse came in and said, "We need to run some tests on you, Mr. Stanley." They wheeled me to several departments for tests, then wheeled me back to my room. A few minutes later, a doctor came in and talked to Liz. I didn't hear what was said, but the next thing I knew, they were getting me ready for surgery. That's when I got scared. Needles and surgery have always scared me, which is why the doctor told Liz what they were going to do.

I asked the nurse, "Why am I having surgery? What happened to me?"

The nurse said, "You had a heart attack, a stroke, and a seizure. We are going to put a stent in your heart." That's all I remember because the medication was kicking in.

When I woke up, Liz and David were in the room with me again. I said, "Why am I here? What happened?"

They told me, and the doctor came into the room. He repeated what had happened, then said, "You're a lucky man, Mr. Stanley. Most people don't survive what you went through. If they do, they have side effects, like paralysis or brain damage." I was a lucky man indeed.

A few days later, I was up and walking. All the medical staff were amazed at what I was doing. They couldn't believe I was moving around as if nothing had happened to me. Then they cleared me to go home.

About a month later, I told Liz what had happened to me when I died. I was a little hesitant to tell her, but something inside me told me I should. To say she was shocked would be an understatement.

I told David as well. We sat at the table many times after this and discussed what I had experienced. Both David and Liz agreed that what I'd experienced was real. They said I should share what I had seen and heard, but there was something inside that said, *Not now.*

About a month or two later, I heard God's voice again. It woke me out of a dead sleep. I lay there, waiting to hear what he would say to me. I prayed while I waited. Then he said, "Share this with everyone, Billy. Don't wait any longer. This message is for everyone."

I said, "Okay, Lord. I will."

∞

This experience brought me closer to God and gave me a clear purpose for the rest of my life. Liz and I were going to church, but my life is much different now. Since my vision of heaven, I have confidence I didn't have before. I know where I'm going when I die, and I'm not afraid to tell anyone that if they believe the gospel with their heart and soul, they are going there too.

It gives me a lot of comfort to do that. God asked me to do this. He gave me a mission as well as the strength to complete it. When I think about heaven, it's the most overwhelming sense of love, joy, and happiness that I've ever experienced. And it's all because of one person, Jesus, and what he did for me. It's real.

After my experience in heaven, I started looking up a lot of near-death experiences online. They're all pretty much the same. Most people talk about going through a tunnel and seeing a bright light. I know what the bright light is. It's him. It's Jesus.

I don't call it a near-death experience anymore. I call it a near-God experience because I was so close to God himself.

This experience taught me a lot of things. One of the unexpected blessings of having a vision of heaven is that you read the Bible with a new set of eyes. The final book of the Bible gives us a stunning picture of heaven and how wonderful it will be:

> Then I saw "a new heaven and a new earth," for the first heaven and the first earth had passed away, and there was no longer any sea. I saw the Holy City, the new Jerusalem, coming down out of heaven from God, prepared as a bride beautifully dressed for her husband. And I heard a loud voice from the throne saying, "Look! God's dwelling place is now among the people, and he will dwell with them. They will be his people, and God himself will be with them and be their God. 'He will wipe every tear from their eyes. There will be no more death' or mourning or crying or pain, for the old order of things has passed away." (Revelation 21:1–4)

Heaven isn't just a story from Sunday school class or some imaginary place concocted by deluded people of faith. Heaven is real. God is there. His Son, Jesus, is real.

These days when I pray, I don't want to ask for anything. All I want to say is, "Thank you, thank you, thank you." I don't have anything left to ask for. God has already given me everything. All I can do is thank him.

Now, of course I'll pray for somebody. If they ask me to pray, or if somebody's sick, I'll pray for them. But my biggest prayer is that God opens their eyes and helps them see it's all true.

TWENTY-SIX

A THING CALLED LOVE

What was it like being Elvis's brother?

That's the question everyone asks me. Anyone who ever knew Elvis has tried to help others understand what it was like, but there aren't enough positive words in the world to describe the experience.

Here is the best I can do to help you understand: The love Elvis projected was so strong, it hit you as soon as you saw him. You knew this man loved you, truly loved you. He didn't care what you did for a living or what color your skin was. He didn't care if you were poor or rich. To me, Elvis had X-ray eyes. He had the uncanny ability to look into your heart and soul.

Elvis radiated love. From his music and creativity, to his generosity and childlike faith, he embodied what the apostle Paul wrote in 1 Corinthians 13, the "love chapter" of the Bible.

> If I speak in the tongues of men or of angels, but do not have love, I
> am only a resounding gong or a clanging cymbal. If I have the gift of
> prophecy and can fathom all mysteries and all knowledge, and if I have

a faith that can move mountains, but do not have love, I am nothing. If I give all I possess to the poor and give over my body to hardship that I may boast, but do not have love, I gain nothing. . . .

When I was a child, I talked like a child, I thought like a child, I reasoned like a child. When I became a man, I put the ways of childhood behind me. For now we see only a reflection as in a mirror; then we shall see face to face. Now I know in part; then I shall know fully, even as I am fully known.

And now these three remain: faith, hope and love. But the greatest of these is love. (vv. 1–3, 11–13)

If anyone had a problem or was in trouble, Elvis would fix it. I saw him help people he didn't know. He didn't do it for publicity. He did it because he cared.

Elvis took what he read in the Bible to heart. It sounds so simple, but he just wanted to be like Christ. When you read the Bible, you will see where Elvis was influenced to be loving and generous. He tried his best to make your day a little better or ease your mind.

The word *love* has lost its meaning today, but it never did in Elvis's world. When he said it, you knew he meant it. Elvis didn't throw the word *love* around. He proved it with his actions. It was so important to him to show how much he cared, not just say it.

When you were around Elvis, you felt loved and safe. He brought a little bit of heaven to earth. Anyone who ever saw him or spent any time with him never forgot the experience. It was forever stuck in your heart and soul.

What do I hope you take away from this book? I hope I have entertained you with these stories from my life with Elvis. I hope you have laughed at some of the crazy situations we got into when I was younger. And I hope you have learned to love and appreciate Elvis more.

But there's something far more important. My hope is that this book brings you closer to God. I have shared a lot of stories and information in these pages. But if I had to boil it all down to just a few lessons we can take away from this journey through Elvis's faith, it would be these three.

1. Don't take life for granted.

From the first time I met Elvis in 1960, I learned that we are not promised tomorrow. We have to make the most of every day, because life is precious. With Elvis, every day was an adventure. He never wasted a moment.

As a kid, I had a hard time trying to keep up with him. When I was with him, we were always on the go. We were always doing something. One day, when I was a little older, I said, "Can I ask you a question, Elvis?"

"Sure. What do you want to know, Billy?"

"Why are you always on the move? Don't you ever get tired? Don't you ever want to slow down a little?"

"That's three questions, Billy." We both laughed; then he continued. "Billy, there's no guarantee for tomorrow. With that in mind, I'm going to live my life like there is no tomorrow. I don't want to waste time while I'm here. I'll slow down when I'm gone."

"But the pace is what I'm talking about. I'm a young guy, and I have a hard time trying to keep up with you."

He gave me that Elvis smile. "The biggest mistake people make in life is taking time for granted. We should all do what we can while we're here. To me, a person who wastes time won't get very far in life. In my book, that's a sin."

I still didn't understand. "But not everyone can keep up with you."

"Everyone has their own pace. It's not a competition, Billy. Just do the best you can at your own pace, and everything will be fine."

From that moment on, I always did my best to make the most of every day.

2. Base your life on the Bible.

Anytime Elvis had a question about how to live or how to deal with a situation, he always went to the Bible. Was he perfect? No, he wasn't. He was human, and he fell short. But Elvis always told me, "Be the best you can be. That's all God expects from anybody. You'll never be perfect, so forget about that, but always try your best."

Elvis didn't believe in doing anything halfway. He believed the Bible called us to live life full-out for God, making the best use of our gifts and talents, and not wasting a moment. Elvis didn't preach at people. He never pulled out a chapter and verse to shove in their faces. He believed it was better to live the gospel rather than just talk about it.

He said, "Everybody should try to be the best person they can be. Don't be a part of the dark side, where the devil is the master of confusion. He's trying to mess with you. Whenever you get those negative thoughts, you know where they're coming from."

Whenever he dealt with self-doubt or anything negative, he would pray. He would question whether he had misread that person. He would meditate about it and try to find something in the Bible that spoke to him. That's where he got his strength.

3. Show God's love to the people around you.

When did it become okay to hate someone just because they don't think or believe the same way you do? That's insane. I remember talking to Elvis one day about this subject. He said, "It would be a dull and boring world if we all thought and believed the same way. That's why God made Ford and Chevrolet."

"Being different is okay," he went on, "and we should accept the fact that not everyone is the same. It's what makes us unique."

To Elvis, *hate* was the worst word you could ever use. He said, "It's the complete opposite of the word *love*." Love is what Elvis was all about.

Elvis dated lots of different women, but the one thing they had in common was that Elvis made each feel like the only woman in the world. That's the way he looked at everyone, not just his romantic partners. His friends and fans saw the love he had for them, and they gave it back to him.

Elvis had his flaws, but millions of people loved him in spite of his shortcomings. That's what God's love is about. No matter what you do, he's still going to love you if you believe in him.

That was the message Elvis wanted to convey in his music. If he were alive today, his hope would be that people would get the meaning of his gospel songs and know that he loved God. Elvis's message to you is that God loves you, he wants you to come to him, and he will help you. That's what it's all about.

God is knocking on your door. Are you going to answer it?

God was using Elvis to reach people through his songs. Did you hear them, and did they mean something to you? Most people will say, "Yes, I heard the meaning," but they don't realize Elvis really believed it too.

That part got me every time. When I was working for him and we would be at a concert, I would scan the crowd during the gospel set. I would wonder to myself, *How many of these people are getting it?* All I could see were people screaming and yelling. They would settle down during the gospel songs, but it was still an Elvis audience, with women trying to get onstage.

Elvis frequently underlined verses in his King James Bible and wrote notes to himself in the margins as a reminder of important truths.

Underneath Psalm 11 he paraphrased verse 1 and wrote, "In the Lord I place my trust and He will guide me."

That is what he wanted his fans to know. He had placed his trust in God, and they could too.

Everyone has a favorite mental picture of Elvis, an image that encapsulates a moment in time we would like to keep forever frozen.

For some fans, it's a black-and-white picture of Elvis as a young man performing on *The Ed Sullivan Show*. For others, it's a scene from an Elvis movie, looming larger than life on the big screen. Still others see Elvis signing autographs with fans, standing with Nixon in the Oval Office, or performing in a white jumpsuit in Vegas.

Here's what I see when I picture Elvis: I see a man who didn't look at the color of someone's skin. I see a man who wasn't afraid to share his belief in God. I see a man who reached out to help everyone and anyone. I see a man who never wanted to let anyone down. I see a man who wasn't afraid to get on his knees and ask for forgiveness. I see a man who loved his family, friends, and fans. I see a man who gave so much of himself that it ended his brief stay on this earth.

The list of what I see could go on and on, but it would take days to complete. You may have noticed that I didn't say a great singer or movie star. Yes, he was both. I've heard all of his records and seen hundreds of concerts. I've seen all of his movies.

Even though I saw all of it, I still don't see Elvis the way you do. I never will. More than anything, I see a man who tried to bring love, joy, compassion, and hope into everyone's life.

That timeless image of Elvis will stay etched in my memory until I get to see him again in heaven. In honor of that memory, I wrote a poem in 2014 that summarizes how I feel about Elvis:

The House on a Hill

There's a house on a hill, in Memphis, Tennessee,
people from around the world come to see.
It belonged to a man, some called him a King.
He was an amazing man, boy could he sing.
He filled the hearts of millions with joy and love.
It was plain to see he was sent from God above.
He loved his fans and his fellow man.
To touch our souls, that was his plan.
He lived a life filled with hopes and dreams.
He was our hero from the movie screens.
One day God called him, took him by the hand.
He said, "It's time to go and leave Graceland."
Elvis asked, "Does this mean that I'm through?"
God said, "Don't worry, my son, they will never forget
about you."

∾

Over the years, hundreds of fans have asked me, "Did Elvis know how much he inspired people?" He knew he had a great gift, but he still loved hearing those words of affirmation we all crave sometimes.

One day Elvis and I were sitting around the house, watching TV. As we were relaxing, I decided to share what I thought about him. I said, "You know what really amazes me about you?"

Elvis looked over at me with a smile. "No, what is it?"

"I love the way you are with people, not just the ones who work for you, or your family, but everyone."

He chuckled. "What do you mean?"

"You are always positive, motivating, and inspirational with everyone you talk to. I've listened to you and watched how you are with people. You make everyone who comes in contact with you feel special. It doesn't matter what they do for a living, you are always the same. They could be dirt poor or rich—it doesn't matter to you because you treat everyone the same. You really do love everyone, and I admire that about you, Elvis."

He looked at me and wiped away a tear. He said, "Come here." I stood up and walked over to him. He put his arms around me; then he said, "That's one of the nicest things anyone has ever said to me, Billy. Thank you."

"I really love you, Elvis. I just wanted you to know why."

He patted my back. "I love you too, Billy."

That was a special moment for Elvis and me, one I'll never forget. To say I'm proud to have spent seventeen years of my life with him is an understatement. Those years are long gone, but the memories are still there. Sometimes it only feels like yesterday when I was with him. Sometimes it feels like it was all a dream.

I've shared my memories of Elvis so you could hear the real story of the man I knew. He was larger-than-life, and so was his faith. This man took me into his family and accepted me as one of his own.

The world will never forget him. Neither will I.

THE FAITH OF ELVIS
DISCUSSION GUIDE

We hope you have enjoyed reading and learning about Elvis's faith and love for God. We don't want your journey to stop there. The greatest tribute you can give to Elvis's legacy of faith is to put these principles into practice in your own life.

You can use the discussion questions below in a variety of ways:

- Use them as journaling prompts in your personal devotion time.
- Read through the book with a group and discuss a set of questions each week.
- Include them as discussion starters in a class, small group, or mastermind where you are engaging with the book.
- Post your answers on social media and invite others to discuss and comment.

However you use them, we hope these questions spur you on to a greater appreciation of Elvis's legacy as well as a deeper love for Jesus.

Introduction

1. What was your impression of Elvis's faith before reading this book?
2. Can you think of any popular recording artists who include gospel music in the middle of their concerts? Why would that seem strange?
3. Billy wrote, "This is what Elvis wanted more than anything: for people to know God and come to faith in Jesus." Would you say that is your greatest desire as well? Why or why not?

Chapter 1: Mansion Over the Hilltop

1. Imagine yourself in Billy and his brothers' shoes that first night at Graceland. How would you have felt?
2. Does it surprise you that Elvis was so excited to become a big brother? Why or why not? How does that differ from the image of Elvis in pop culture?
3. Elvis made Billy and his brothers feel special, needed, and wanted that first night when he prayed with them. Is there someone in your life you are praying for in the same way?
4. James 1:22–24 talks about not being just a listener to the Word, but a doer of it. How did Elvis put God's Word into practice by welcoming Billy and his brothers into his life?

Chapter 2: He Knows Just What I Need

1. Billy wrote, "The person you saw on the screen or at concerts was the same person you saw at Graceland. Elvis was every bit of the fun-loving, warm, caring person you'd expect him to be, and then some." Did this statement surprise you? Why or why not?
2. Elvis felt so close to God that God knew his name, and Elvis knew

God's. If someone asked you what it meant to be close to God, how would you explain it?

3. Billy wrote that faith was one of the many gifts Elvis gave him. Who helped give *you* the gift of faith? Is there someone in your life whose faith you are helping to develop?

4. Proverbs 6:22 says, "When you walk, they will guide you; when you sleep, they will watch over you; when you awake, they will speak to you." The Word of God guided and changed Elvis's and Billy's lives. How is God's Word guiding and speaking to you now?

Chapter 3: You'll Never Walk Alone

1. Billy learned to think bigger in the setting of family and laughter. How important is a sense of security and fun to a child's healthy development?

2. Elvis told Billy, "Don't worry about failing. If you don't accomplish what you set out to do, be proud that you gave it everything you had, that you left nothing to chance." Why is this important advice for a young person?

3. How would you have felt in Billy's shoes when he was getting musical advice from Elvis? Who in your life has helped you gain confidence in your creative abilities?

Chapter 4: In My Father's House

1. Why is it so important to have a steady father figure in a young man's life?

2. Proverbs 1:8–9 says, "Listen, my son, to your father's instruction and do not forsake your mother's teaching. They are a garland to grace your head and a chain to adorn your neck." What is the most important thing your mother or father taught you?

3. Do you think it was hard for Vernon to become a father figure to three young boys who were not biologically his own? Why or why not?

4. Describe a few ways you try to make your home a safe and welcoming place for your family.

Chapter 5: Somebody Bigger Than You and I

1. Put yourself in Billy's shoes. What would it have been like to be part of a new family and discover that your new brother was world-famous?

2. First Peter 5:6–7 says, "Humble yourselves, therefore, under God's mighty hand, that he may lift you up in due time. Cast all your anxiety on him because he cares for you." What are the challenges to staying humble when you are famous?

3. Elvis felt his career was just a job like any other person had. How did this view help keep him humble and grounded?

4. Who is the most famous person you have ever met? Did you get the sense that he or she was grounded and humble? Why or why not?

Chapter 6: I'll Be Home for Christmas

1. If you were in Elvis's shoes and had access to virtually anything you wanted, would it be difficult to keep the focus on Jesus during Christmas? Why or why not?

2. What is the most meaningful Christmas gift you ever received? What made it special?

3. How do you try to keep the focus on Jesus during the Christmas season?

4. Titus 3:4–5 says, "But when the kindness and love of God our Savior appeared, he saved us, not because of righteous things we had done, but because of his mercy." As you are reading Billy's story, do you see ways Elvis showed God's kindness and love to him and his brothers?

5. Billy wrote, "The only difference between Christmas and any other day with Elvis was that we had a tree at Christmas." What is something simple you can do to make someone else's day "like Christmas" today?

Chapter 7: It Is No Secret (What God Can Do)

1. Does it surprise you that Elvis only won Grammy Awards for his gospel music?

2. In this chapter, Billy emphasizes that Elvis saw his gospel music not as a performance, but as a calling and a ministry. He writes, "Elvis saw himself as a gospel singer who just happened to sing rock and roll and star in movies." How does this change your view of Elvis?

3. Near Psalm 137 in his Bible, Elvis wrote, "The highest graces of music flow from the feelings of the heart-soul." How does music draw you closer to God? Are there any particular gospel songs by Elvis that you love?

4. Do you view your career or vocation as a calling from God? Why or why not?

Chapter 8: He Touched Me

1. Proverbs 11:25 says, "A generous person will prosper; whoever refreshes others will be refreshed." What are some ways the Lord has refreshed you when you have been generous to others?

2. Elvis wrote in his Bible, "If one can't give what they have and share then they will always be empty." Why did giving seem to make Elvis so happy?

3. Billy told a story about Elvis giving money to a complete stranger on the street. Have you ever given money to a stranger? What happened as a result?

4. Think of people who have been generous to you. How did it change or improve your life? How did it increase your faith?

5. Second Corinthians 9:7 says, "God loves a cheerful giver." Why does God love it when a person gives cheerfully?

Chapter 9: Oh Happy Day

1. Colossians 3:23–24 says: "Whatever you do, work at it with all your heart, as working for the Lord, not for human masters, since you know that you will receive an inheritance from the Lord as a reward. It is the Lord Christ you are serving." What are some ways you work at your job or position with all your heart? How do you try to honor the Lord through it?

2. Elvis truly loved his fans. Does it change your perspective of his music, knowing that he had such a deep appreciation for his fans?

3. Billy wrote that Elvis "would always take the conversation off him and put it onto the other person." How do you think this made the other person feel? Is it harder for us to give our full attention to someone today than it was in Elvis's time?

Chapter 10: Where No One Stands Alone

1. John 13:34 says, "A new command I give you: Love one another. As I have loved you, so you must love one another." Elvis lived out this

command by standing up to racial injustice and by treating others equally. What are three ways you can live out this command in your own life?

2. If Elvis had gotten to meet Martin Luther King Jr., what do you think they would have talked about?

3. Billy wrote, "Elvis didn't care where you were from or who you were. He treated everybody who worked for him the same." Do you treat everyone in your care the same, whether family, employees, or team members?

Chapter 11: By and By

1. Did it surprise you to learn that Elvis wanted to be done with making movies and get back to performing live concerts? Why or why not?

2. Even though Elvis wanted to be done with making movies long before he was, he honored his contracts. Is there a difficult situation you are dealing with right now that requires patience? How can you act with integrity and honor your commitments while still aiming for your goals?

3. Elvis wrote a note to himself in his Bible. It said, "There is a season for everything, patience will reward you and reveal the answers to your questions." As you look back on challenging situations in your past, how did patience reward you?

4. Isaiah 40:30–31 says, "Even youths grow tired and weary, and young men stumble and fall; but those who hope in the LORD will renew their strength." How did you see the Lord renewing Elvis's strength during this period of his life?

Chapter 12: Stand by Me

1. How does a Christian balance Jesus' command to "turn the other cheek" with the need to stand up to bullies by using force (see Matthew 5:38–40)?
2. Proverbs 17:17 says, "A friend loves at all times, and a brother is born for a time of adversity." Who is a "brother" or "sister" you can call on when times get tough?
3. Has anyone ever stood up for you? How did it make you feel?
4. How have you stood up for others who were being bullied or mistreated?

Chapter 13: I've Got Confidence

1. Elvis took special care to train and mentor Billy. How do you see a similar mentoring relationship played out in stories from the Bible, such as Paul and Timothy, Jesus and the disciples, or Moses and Joshua?
2. Proverbs 13:20 says, "Walk with the wise and become wise, for a companion of fools suffers harm." Who in your inner circle is wise? How can you spend more time with them?
3. Think of one or two people who gave you confidence and skills in your vocation or career. What specific ways did they help you grow as a person or leader?

Chapter 14: Swing Down, Sweet Chariot

1. Elvis and Billy bonded over driving fast cars. Think about someone in your life whom you are mentoring or teaching. What hobby or activity do you use to strengthen your bond and provide learning experiences?

2. Proverbs 27:17 says, "As iron sharpens iron, so one person sharpens another." Who are you "sharpening"? How are you making that person better?

3. After hearing Billy's experience getting into a fast car with Elvis, would you have liked to ride along? Why or why not?

4. What can we learn about respecting law enforcement from the story of Elvis getting pulled over by the policeman?

Chapter 15: Lead Me, Guide Me

1. Billy wrote, "Much of what has been said and written over the years about Elvis's philandering has been overblown to the extent that it has in some ways defined who he was. This is not a fair way to look at anyone's life." None of us want to be defined by our mistakes. Why do we seem so quick to do this to celebrities?

2. Matthew 7:1–2 says, "Do not judge, or you too will be judged. For in the same way you judge others, you will be judged, and with the measure you use, it will be measured to you." How do these verses help you stay away from judging others inappropriately?

3. Elvis wrote in his Bible, "To judge a man by his weakest link or deed is like judging the power of the ocean by one wave." What is your "weakest link"? Would you want the world to define you by that one aspect of your life?

4. Is there an area of your life where you're currently struggling with sin? How can you let God's grace into your heart to cover over your guilt and shame?

Chapter 16: If the Lord Wasn't Walking by My Side

1. Have you ever faced a situation like the one described at the beginning of the chapter, where Elvis dealt with the unruly diner customer? How did Elvis show his love for people by protecting them from harm in various situations?

2. Elvis often wrote reminders or Scripture verses in the margins of his Bible, such as "Lord send me light to guide me" and "Trust in the Lord not man." Describe a current situation in your life where you need God's light and wisdom. Have you asked God for guidance?

3. Romans 12:17–18 says, "Do not repay anyone evil for evil. Be careful to do what is right in the eyes of everyone. If it is possible, as far as it depends on you, live at peace with everyone." Is there someone in your life who has done you harm? How can you attempt to live at peace with them instead of repaying them for what they have done?

Chapter 17: America, the Beautiful

1. Elvis said, "That's why it's so important that your generation keeps God as the foundation of our great country, Billy. Never lose that." What does it mean in practical ways to keep God as the foundation of a country?

2. Romans 13:1 says, "Let everyone be subject to the governing authorities, for there is no authority except that which God has established." How should a Christian respond when the governing authorities don't follow godly principles? What would Elvis do in this situation?

3. Elvis believed that the purpose of music was not to make political statements. Do you agree or disagree? Why?

Chapter 18: Run On

1. Did you previously know about the story of Elvis getting a DEA badge? If not, what was your reaction to learning about it?

2. Elvis said, "All my heroes wear uniforms." Who is someone in your life who wears a uniform, and what do you admire about them?

3. James 2 talks about the importance of both faith and deeds. Think over your activities and schedule from this past week. How have you shown your faith by your actions, your calendar, and your priorities? How can you show your faith by your deeds over the coming week?

4. Billy referred to the industry of Elvis tribute artists—otherwise known as Elvis impersonators. If there were tribute artists dedicated to *your* life, what would they look or sound like? What personality or character qualities would they try to highlight?

Chapter 19: How Great Thou Art

1. Romans 1:16 says, "For I am not ashamed of the gospel, because it is the power of God that brings salvation to everyone who believes: first to the Jew, then to the Gentile." Elvis tried to put this idea into practice through singing gospel music. How can you put it into practice in your life? How can you make the gospel known through your vocation, reputation, or relationships?

2. It was, and still is, very unusual for a rock or pop artist to perform gospel songs in his or her shows. How do you think people would respond to that if Elvis were alive and making music today?

3. Elvis believed spiritual truth could come through "secular" songs such as "Bridge over Troubled Water." What non-gospel songs do you enjoy that have a deep spiritual meaning to you?

Chapter 20: Amazing Grace

1. This chapter mentioned the parable of the talents, found in Matthew 25. What is the biggest talent or skill God has given you? How can you use it for his glory?

2. Since you're reading this book, you are likely an Elvis fan. As you have listened to his music over the years, did you get a clear sense of the message of God's love coming through?

3. Billy wrote, "Elvis was the same person onstage and off. There was no difference." That is a remarkable statement, since Elvis was the biggest celebrity of his time. Could people say the same thing about you—that you are the same person in your public and private lives?

4. John 16:33 says, "I have told you these things, so that in me you may have peace. In this world you will have trouble. But take heart! I have overcome the world." God can comfort you in your troubles, just as he helped Elvis. What strength or comfort do you need to ask God for today?

Chapter 21: Help Me

1. Elvis was concerned that he stay spiritually grounded even while he was a wealthy celebrity. He wrote in his Bible, "For what is a man advantaged, if he gain the whole world, and lose himself, or be cast away" (quoting Luke 9:25 KJV). How do you stay grounded in your faith while also living in a time of unprecedented wealth and material abundance?

2. Billy wrote, "Elvis just took it all in stride and didn't get hung up on what people did to him. He didn't keep emotional scorecards, on other people or himself." Do you tend to keep emotional scorecards on those who have hurt you? Be honest.

3. Imagine yourself in Elvis's shoes. How might you have handled the fame, power, and wealth? Where would you have been the most tempted?

Chapter 22: Farther Along

1. Like Paul in Philippians 3:8, do you consider "everything a loss" compared to the "surpassing worth of knowing Christ Jesus"? What makes it so hard sometimes to value our relationship with Christ above all else?
2. How do you know when you are drawing closer to God? Be specific.
3. Elvis dealt with many obstacles to his faith and success. One of them was Colonel Parker, who gave him his big break as a young performer but became a liability as the years went on. Is there anyone in your life that you consider an obstacle? How would God have you handle this situation?
4. How would you have responded if Elvis had asked *you* to be the one to share his real story? Would it feel like an immense pressure? A great responsibility? A huge honor? All three?

Chapter 23: Known Only to Him

1. Billy said, "[Elvis] taught me that life is a gift from God. We should thank God for that every day. When we're gone, we're gone. There is no encore, so we have to do what we can do while we're here on this earth." How does this inspire you to live every day to its fullest?
2. How did you respond to the story of Elvis's mother's ghost walking around Graceland?

3. Think about a loved one in your life. If you knew today was the last time you would speak with him or her, what would you say?

4. Psalm 90:12 says, "Teach us to number our days, that we may gain a heart of wisdom." When you understand that your time on earth is limited, how does it help you be wise in how you spend your time?

Chapter 24: If We Never Meet Again

1. Have you ever lost someone close to you unexpectedly? Who helped comfort you on that day?

2. Can you picture an older Elvis? What might he look like? What kind of music or entertainment might he be making if he were still alive?

3. In the margin of his Bible, Elvis copied Psalms 46:10, which says, "Be still, and know that I am God." How does "being still" help us have peace in times of grief, stress, or sadness?

Chapter 25: Seeing Is Believing

1. How did you respond to Billy's account of seeing Elvis in heaven? Have you ever had such an experience, or known someone who has?

2. Several people in Billy's life, including his wife, Liz, and his brothers, Rick and David, were instrumental in bringing him back to the Lord. Who has had the most influence in your life, helping you have a strong relationship with Jesus? Have you told them how they impacted you?

3. How do the words from Revelation 21 about "a new heaven and a new earth" give you comfort and peace concerning what God has prepared for us?

Chapter 26: A Thing Called Love

1. In 1 Corinthians 13:13, Paul wrote, "And now these three remain: faith, hope and love. But the greatest of these is love." When your closest friends and family think of your life, would *love* be one of the first words they would associate with you? Why or why not?

2. Do you take life for granted, or do you make the most of every day? Be honest.

3. Billy once told Elvis, "You are always positive, motivating, and inspirational with everyone you talk to. I've listened to you and watched how you are with people. You make everyone who comes in contact with you feel special." Is there someone in your life who makes you feel the same way? Have you told them so?

ACKNOWLEDGMENTS

First and foremost, thanks to Elvis. You showed me a life that most people can only dream about. I am grateful that you opened your home and treated me like a brother.

Thanks to Rick and David for being my brothers and supporting me every step of the way.

Thanks to my mother for always making sure I was in church.

Thanks to Ashley and Emily for saving my life.

Thanks to the Elvis fans for always being there.

Thanks to Kent Sanders for helping tell the story of Elvis's faith.

Thanks to Liz for being the angel God placed in my life. Since I've been with you, I have believed in angels, because you are perfect for me.

And most of all, thanks to God for never giving up on me. You waited for me a long time, but I finally came around. I am eternally grateful for your love and grace.

NOTES

1. "Walter Matthau: Biography," IMDb, accessed May 4, 2022, https://www.imdb.com/name/nm0000527/bio.

2. George C. Scott, as General George S. Patton, in *Patton* (film), directed by Franklin J. Schaffner (Los Angeles: 20th Century Fox, 1970).

3. Exec. Order No. 11,085, 28 F.R. 1759 (1963).

4. Frank Sinatra, "My Way," music by Claude François, lyrics by Gilles Thibaut, Jacques Revaux, and Paul Anka, in *My Way*, Reprise, 1969, album.

ABOUT THE AUTHORS

Billy Stanley is a *New York Times* bestselling author and the stepbrother of Elvis Presley. As one of the singer's trusted confidants, Stanley witnessed Elvis's faith in action firsthand. A successful salesman and former airplane mechanic, Stanley and his wife, Liz, live in Memphis, Tennessee, just a few miles from Graceland.

Kent Sanders is the author or coauthor of several books, including *18 Words to Live By*, *The Daily Writer*, and *The Artist's Suitcase*. He is also host of the *Daily Writer* podcast, which helps writers cultivate habits for success. He lives outside of St. Louis with his wife and son.